77

COVER ART: Claire Boyle.

INTERIOR ILLUSTRATIONS: Dongyan Xu.

COVER LETTERING: Lauren Tamaki.

Printed in Canada

This project is supported in part by the National Endowment for the Arts. To find out more about how National Endowment for the Arts grants impact individuals and communities, visit www.arts.gov.

DEAR MCSWEENEY'S,

Soon I'll be a divorcée. In six weeks and a day. The divorce decree has been granted. That's how the paperwork describes itself: "decree, granted." Now there's just an on-tenterhooks time when either of us could change our minds, write to the court, and undo it all, no matter what the other one thinks, which seems old-fashioned and, frankly, regressive. Shouldn't staying married depend on the will of the person who wants to be married less, not more? Not that either of us will do that. We split up years ago, but paperwork is boring, and the lack of official permission to consider ourselves unmarried didn't affect our lives. We didn't have to disentangle children or property. We weren't even in the same country.

We got married in the United States, where I live, but we're getting divorced in England, where he (my soon-to-be-or-possibly-already-ex-husband) lives. Easier and cheaper, it turns out. When we filed, I didn't know I'd be spending part of July and all of August on the southeastern coast of England, just forty miles down the road from his home. We haven't seen each other. We won't. I think I'm supposed to think this is sad, but I don't. I'm glad neither of us feels as if the shared past has to pressure us into some version of a shared future.

I'm staying in a house in the English equivalent of a state park. The house sits almost as close as you can get to the edge of a cliff without sliding over it. In the adjacent lot, behind some brambles and barbed wire, there's a radar station that was erected during the Second World War. The visible part of the radar station looks like a helicopter rotor mounted on a metal pole. As it rotates, it emits a constant low hum, like a swarm of bees, though it's more regular, because it's mechanized, and in its regularity there's a strange music. Walkers coming to the park pass by my windows in all weather, and stare at me as if I am myself a natural feature. Which makes sense. It's an odd place for a house. The other day a woman knocked on my door close to sunset. "Are you one of the people who watch over the cliffs?" she asked. I said yes, and then no, once I realized she meant the Coast Guard, someone official, not just a woman with windows and proximity. It didn't seem to matter; she passed along her news—a boat looked to be in trouble—and then disappeared down the path while I was getting my boots and binoculars.

It's been a summer of strange affinities and loneliness, this summer of divorcing. I left New York to spend a month in Maui. Lived in a house in an eighteen-acre palm forest. No Wi-Fi or cell service. I saw Walter, the gardener, more than any other person. No one seemed to know his age, but he had white hair and was certainly over sixty, and spry. Sometimes, from my desk, I'd see his head bobbing through the fronds and flowers as he jogged uphill. He was born in Germany, and spoke English with a German accent. He hadn't been back there since he'd moved to California, and then to Hawaii, following a guru, decades before. He played classical guitar. He had a famously beautiful lover. Mosquitoes no longer troubled him. He'd become an expert on palm trees by accident; he saw the job advertised, and he took it. Now he knows this forest better than anyone else.

He took me on walks, showed me his favorite meditation spots, and smiled at my questions, like you'd smile at a child. "Isn't this a lot to garden?" I said. "It is not a garden," he answered. "It is a forest." When we said goodbye, I gave him my book; he gave me a CD on which he plays classical guitar as backup for a woman singing ancient Japanese poems.

Here in England, the closest thing I have to a friend is Dani, the nineteen-year-old server at the village pub that's only a half hour's walk over the Firehills. She's got long blond hair that looks like a wig in a fantasy movie, and an earnest affect. Everything she says sounds urgent. I overtip her habitually, after doing it once accidentally. I don't go to the pub every day I might wish to, even if I'm feeling lonely, in order to preserve both familiarity and mystery. I'm titrating intimacy.

This morning I woke up and emailed my ex to ask if he'd heard from the courts, as it seemed like about the right time for them to have responded to the divorce petition. He wrote back immediately: "The decree literally just came in the mail and I was just starting to write to you when your message came in. Freaky." Then he told me about the six weeks and a day. Honestly, I'm charmed by that one more day. That's fairy-tale time. Spell-time. I think it's fitting. Getting married is spell-work—*I do*, language transforming reality, converted into boredom and tax breaks by God and bureaucracy—and getting out of it should have some attendant glamour. Like saying *I'm a divorcée*, so preferable to *I'm divorced*.

Walter, Dani, my husband who won't be anymore: all people I know and don't know at all. Again, I think I'm supposed to find this sad, everything I can't understand about people in general and in particular, but I really find it marvelous that I can feel affection for such different people, that the affection can take such varied forms, that intimacy can be true and present—and then pass away, without any negation of its past. There was a time, several years ago now, when I hated my husband as much as I'd once loved him, and every conversation we had became litigation. It's wonderful to realize that hate can wane like love, and in place of both can emerge a cordial indifference.

When I went out to the cliff's edge after the woman came to my door, I saw what she'd alerted me to a small boat drifting out to sea, and steadily east with the wind. There were two dots in it that were probably people. No sails. No wake. The sun was setting. I thought about how embarrassing it would be to call the Coast Guard for a false alarm. Then I thought that if I were in that boat, and in trouble, I'd want someone looking at me from a place of greater safety to care

more about me than the possibility of minor humiliation.

Sincerely,

ELISA GONZALEZ
FAIRLIGHT, ENGLAND

DEAR MCSWEENEY'S,
I never review books. The first rule of survival in the literary rat barrel: never say a negative word about a living writer. Does Elena Ferrante count as living? I did sort of review her recently in some emails. You know Jan Wilm, right? His novel *Winterjahrbuch* is a German classic, starting right about page 180 of 453. Here is our conversation:

DEAR NELL,
You should give Ferrante's *The Lost Daughter* a try, if you don't know it yet. I think it's really well done, and it deals with (female) psychology in a very interesting way.

JAN

DEAR JAN,
I read the first of the four Neapolitan novels and kept thinking the author was definitely a man. Now I can't remember what the tells were, but it was a rollicking good story about those virgin/whore

space aliens whose exteriors we
all know and love. Of course
that's no reason for a woman not
to have written it. But I wasn't
blown away. My pal Johanna
lent me *The Lost Daughter*
months ago and I got bored and
stopped reading it. Will pick it
up again.

NELL

DEAR NELL,
I'm convinced that Ferrante is
a woman and a man, a couple
writing those books together
like Sjöwall and Wahlöö, or
however the fuck you spell that
Swedish-crime-novel couple.
Anita Raja, a translator from
the German, and Domenico
Starnone, a novelist. I read
one other book by Starnone:
Trick (a good book!). For years
people believed he was Ferrante
(before that hack journalist
revealed Ferrante was probably
Raja), and the style and tone
are very similar, even though
Starnone and Ferrante have
different translators. I'm usually
skeptical of "male style" and
"female style," or whatever
people call those markers of
feminine-v.-masculine prose
and worldviews, but I believe
that part of the appeal (not to
me!) of Ferrante is precisely that

feeling that people think it's
written by a man, while they
convince themselves that it was
written by a woman because—
whoa!—it has a woman's name
on the cover. I liked the book
immensely, also because it
involves the kind of pointless
theft of a doll, which I fucking
loved, and a tiny sliver of self-
deprecating academia-bashing,
which is always good fun. Plus
it has a killer last line. I'm
surprised you find it boring.
I read it in an afternoon and
found it a (God, I hate the
word) page-turner. Back to the
Paella factory, i.e., the novel.

JAN

DEAR JAN,
Still seems to me like a tableau
vivant by a Freudian who's read
a lot about women, watched
them, and found them either
revolting or sexy, depending
on their looks, but has never
been one,* and, either way, the
moral to the story ("unnatural
mother") isn't exactly progressive. But the character never
progresses; she's damaged and
stuck forever, and a harridan
besides. *e.g. she says her
daughter was taller than her by
age sixteen, when some girls
reach almost their full height at

twelve and virtually all are done
growing by sixteen; it's boys
who have a growth spurt after
puberty!

NELL

DEAR NELL,
I agree with most of what
you're saying (especially that
Freudianism is kind of vomited
all over this book), except the
implication that literature needs
in some way to be progressive.
And of course my French-theory
background makes me squirm
when inferring too much
about the author via seemingly
implausible details. Life and
literature are more varied,
I find, than fixed rules without
exceptions might make us
believe. Maybe you just didn't
like it. I streamed the film
adaptation the other day, which
is often laughable, but it has
the great Olivia Colman in it,
and it tweaks something I find
very funny: the Neapolitans
become nouveau-riche lowlifes
from Queens.
    Xo
JAN

DEAR JAN,
The way the kids tyrannize her
because someone else is too nice
to them is also very Schwarze

[archconservative] Pädagogik...
It's a fine book! Just happens to
be one of those where I think,
No wonder people like it,
it's chock-full of a foolproof
secret ingredient: insidiously
misogynistic and snobby
social-climbing guilt. Not saying that about you; you're one
of those young, naive formalists.
You'll come around to wanting agitprop one of these days.
I'd rather see an author try to
better the world and fail. But,
come on, she even sleeps her
way to the top...

NELL

DEAR NELL,
Yeah, totally, I'm not
disagreeing with anything
you say. And like I implied
in a previous email, there is
a savage streak in contemporary
phallocentric culture or (post-)
post-phallocentric/post-feminist
culture (which, sum total, are
almost the same thing, but then
I was never convinced that the
watered-down feminism of the
third wave was useful, except
for some minor improvements
by way of intersectionality,
which has its own problems,
of course), which allows even
women to read a book by an
author with a female name

that features a terrible woman as a central character and go: *Wow, this is so clever! She's writing about how horrible we are.* From a feminist point of view, this is almost worse than outright misogyny, because the male projection has taken root. Discursively, this is all fascinating, almost regardless of what's happening in the novel—*aber das steht auf einem anderen Blatt.* Having said that, I thought the character was very well done, because there is a deep sadness and self-hatred in the subtext. Narratively, the stab at the end is well done and all, but it could, of course, be seen as a very simplistic way of doing Freud, being both phallic and cathartic because of being self-mutilating by proxy. I thought the academia sleeping-to-the-top thing was a nice touch—not that she *does* sleep her way to the top, which is old hat and a bit silly in contemporary literature (well, this is from 2006 or something, so it's almost twenty years old), but the way her professor suddenly wants to benefit from her by introducing her to the Hardy character, and the Hardy character asking to be seated at her table because she's

a good-looking young woman, something he never would have done if she were a man. In the film, this becomes cartoonishly bad, but to me, this is one of the best parts of the novel. Ha, I'm not against agitprop if it has aesthetic value (most of it does not, of course)—but all that matters is the Kipling phrase from "The Conundrum of the Workshops": "It's pretty, but is it Art?" Have you read Lydia Millet's *Dinosaurs*? It tries to do something interesting with a character who tries to "save the world." I had to do a report for a publisher on it. See the book attached.

   Xo

JAN

And now we're on to Millet!
   Hoping for a rising tide that raises all rats,

NELL ZINK
BAD BELZIG, GERMANY

DEAR MCSWEENEY'S,
I'm writing this from the back seat of a robot car. Gliding home in one of these cars after a night out is one of my favorite things to do right now. It may surprise you to learn this—it sure came as a surprise to me—since I love nothing

more than responding to new technology with skepticism. And, let's face it, a skeptical response to any new technology coming out of San Francisco has never failed anyone with the discipline to maintain it over decades of revolutions, protocol wars, network effects, unicorns, hyperobjects, supercycles, and platform decay. It always ends with a handful of guys, nearly all of them white, becoming incredibly rich and extremely patronizing while everyone else is left holding the bag.

But here I am! I giggled with glee as tonight's Waymo One pulled up to the curb with a massive Light Detection and Ranging sensor whirring on its roof. I slid into the right-side passenger seat. Sitting as far away from the "driver" as I possibly can just feels like the polite thing to do, and I've never been able to shake the habit of minding my manners. (I even start my ChatGPT prompts with "please.")

I buckled my seat belt—if you don't buckle up, another sensor will beep at you, because of course the robots are narcs on top of everything else. Now the car's spa-like music is swelling around me. You can choose your own music station, or cast music from your phone, but trying to control the

experience is a rookie move, a clear sign that you've miscalculated the entire situation. And I'm sunk way back into the plush leather seat of the Jaguar I-PACE model so I have the best view of the steering wheel while the car spins me over the hills of San Francisco.

Before I started riding, the steering wheels were what early adopters had told me the most about. (Add early adopters to my list of reasons for reflexive skepticism—they never shut up about their new toys.) The early adopters all loved their robot car rides, of course. Such smooth acceleration! So much caution at intersections! So much excitement at being chauffeured straight into the future!

Except for those steering wheels. With every lane change, turn, acceleration, and deceleration, the steering wheel spins, pulses, and twitches in front of the empty driver's seat. It looks like it's still being guided by human hands. The early adopters would always note this with a touch of discomfort, like the uncanny valley would yawn open beneath their feet as soon as they conjured the memory. From acquaintances who worked at Waymo, I'd also heard of cryptic plans to replace the ghost-in-the-wheel with a solid box on the dashboard that didn't move. Based on all the bellyaching, I assumed I'd also be repulsed when I took my first ride. Instead, I love the wheel. I'm staring at it right now with a small, beatific smile.

The wheel is what makes the experience of the robot car not only manageable but desirable. Think about it this way, McSweeney's: As a metaphor, the robot car writes itself. We sit in the back, strapped in for dear life, while unseen forces turn and burn us through space. We watch, helpless to change anything, as something we can't see and can barely comprehend steers us toward a target in the deep distance.

Disempowerment and disembodiment are the ultimate goals of the past several decades' worth of consumer technology, and the robot cars function as precise experiences of those conditions. It's not always bad to be disempowered and disembodied. Those news reports about people having sex in the backs of robot cars show how abandoning our agency and control can make us feel giddy—how, with a few more personal responsibilities left incomplete, a few more immediate needs moved out of our reach, we can try new ways of getting away with something (even if that something means trying,

desperately, to get back into our bodies).

And as much as disempowerment and disembodiment are long-term causes of unhappiness and distress, they can be of great relief in the short term. Since I live in San Francisco in 2024, they're familiar companions, sad but necessary elements of my daily tool kit. My days are spent "hustling," "grinding," and "girlbossing" to keep the bills paid among two types of people: those who have been granted, as their natural right, assistance from the state and the public to extract data, attention, and resources from all who surround them; and those whose states of extreme mental and physical deterioration have resulted in no help, no favor, and no mercy. You'd better believe I don't feel empowered here. You'd better believe I'm dissociating from something or someone every single day.

And there is no more gentle, frictionless, or elegant way to achieve disempowerment and disembodiment than signing up for the robot car's easy modulations over the landscape, its promise of a human-free future path from point A to point B.

The only wrinkle is the wheel. With its visible agitation, its whirling-dervish movements, its frightening *em*bodiment, the wheel threatens to throw the whole thing off. It's interrupting the flow, eddying the stream. I can't take my eyes off it, because it reminds me that my senses are still alive, no matter how capable I can be at banishing them. It's prodding me to remember what my true role in all this is: not to act out against the machine by behaving badly in the back seat, nor to float out of my body in complete submission to it. The wheel is a reminder that I still have directions to choose, decisions to make, and duties to uphold. No wonder it scares so many riders.

See you at the next stop,

CAILLE MILLNER
SAN FRANCISCO, CA

DEAR MCSWEENEY'S,
Once, in my early twenties, after moving to the country's interior, I put on an old pair of black ankle boots my father had bought me when I was a teenager, and that I had stored for several years in a plastic bag, and halfway to campus the thick rubber sole began crumbling into pieces that left my gait uneven. I looked down, surprised to see that I had been leaving a trail of dark fragments, small and decaying, with every step on the pavement.

I share this with you, bearing in mind how Édouard Glissant describes totality as being revealed through "the accumulation of sediments." So when I say I moved in my early twenties to a small Midwestern town in order to study the accumulation of language, which is my voice, then you will know that I mean there was debris: the apartment, half-underground, at the edge of town; the boy I had married one week prior, whom I had known since childhood within our immigrant fold; how we tried to start our life together in a swallowed geography; how one day afterward I would return to this empty field and attempt to map the geometry of my murky body, the estranged spot in its mouth, its soundless navigations in the nocturnal dark.

Debris: After we were married, we moved to the Midwest, where the wind carried the smell of nearby farmlands and the air was filled with tiny insects. In the Midwest, small winged bugs kept flying into my eyelashes; I could feel them when I blinked.

Debris: If I store it in the body like a grocery list. If I store it in the body like how weather absorbs into the skin. If it becomes part of my fingers, always in startled gestures; or my shadow, consistently taller, more insistent than my actual limbs. If the body has no language, I will draw circles like bruises of clouds.

Debris: When I was a child in Texas, I was like a tempest at home but mostly mute in school or places outside the house. Outside the house, I trembled with fear, humiliation, and anger, though I hardly knew about what, exactly.

Here is a collection of random arcs of naming found in *The Melancholy of Race: Psychoanalysis, Assimilation, and Hidden Grief*, a critical text by cultural theorist Anne Anlin Cheng: *alien body, assimilated body, mis-speaking body, obscene body, diseased body, morbid body, mediating body, buried body, porous body, body-within-body*. Here is a small sequence of photographs, diagrams, illustrations: a faded sepia square of my mother as a child, her face gravelly and creased in the corner; one of my silhouette in the doorway of my grandparents' Mei Foo apartment just as it begins to rain; a Xerox of a linguistics schematic depicting the throat at various stages of vocalization, edged by a black rectangle of inverted light. Here, finally, is a handful of tiny seashells I have gathered from the coast that

are too small to sound when you hold them to your ear.

Fractures of earth, estrangements of sky, things buried, subterranean, missing, decomposing: for at the bottom of the deep ocean, where darkness is a shroud against a world occluded by miles lost underneath the light, the seafloor is an accumulation of sediments comprising fossil remains of tiny microscopic creatures called radiolaria. Barely matter, these single-celled organisms drifted stochastically, ubiquitously, across ancient and modern waters, carried by the currents, which is to say, wind, heat, salt, the moon. What I love about radiolaria is how infinitesimal and insignificant they are—fractions beyond even the tiniest broken shells on my shelf—hidden among other tangential invisibilities like weather and the slow adjustment of tectonic plates. What I love is how, close-up, they are spiny, barbed creatures with a prickly resemblance to stars.

How, then, can I not imagine these asterisked dust motes as windblown migrants, lost in the overwhelming mouth of an endless sea, perforated by their volatile environment, yet somehow insistent on accumulating mass? For the wildest astonishment about radiolaria is how they literally conjure their bodies out of the surrounding debris. Drifting along, they slowly amass intricate mineral skeletons of multitudinous patterns, globular shells full of holes through which to stretch little, soft limbs where they do not actually own any, in order to catch whatever sustenance floats within their grasp.

It is all but silent in the margin of the deep where they now sleep, referred to as the abyssal zone—*abyss*, incidentally, being a word Glissant uses in reference to the dark and impenetrable sea of history, that site of unknowable devastation, dispossession, and ever-shifting ongoingness. In the abyssal zone, our dead and decaying float back down to us as snow falling across swollen borders. Like history, what is opaque comes to us in fragments, gathering itself as it falls. The seafloor accumulates in layers of ooze rising up to meet us. Specks of detritus fall into our eyelids; we can never acknowledge how saturated we are.

Dear McSweeney's, would a pinpricked array as wide as the sky cast long shadows in light of lost constellations? If I exhale with exquisite slowness, might something of matter appear in the form of gravitational condensation? Debris: we do not go

blinking in the dark; we watch for our bones to take up space; we tremble our bodies to become an atmosphere.

In relation,

JENNIFER S. CHENG
SAN FRANCISCO, CA

DEAR MCSWEENEY'S,
This is the best hotel in Las Vegas because you can't tell that you're in Las Vegas. You aren't forced to walk through a casino to get anywhere—no flashing lights, no ringing bells, no disorienting carpets. Not glitzy or garish at all! No naked poker dealers in thongs lined up at the plate glass window like at Caesars Palace—a gynecological experience you were not necessarily expecting to have while ferrying your luggage to the elevator bank. No, no. At this sedate hotel, the most Vegas you get is insipid EDM playing everywhere. But you'd find that at a trendy Tulsa hotel, too.

The last time I was in Las Vegas, you'll remember, was with you for that pre-pandemic Believer Festival for your sibling publication, *The Believer*. Miranda July had all of us submit our sexual fantasies, which she read out loud from the stage, first admonishing us not to laugh. I was unhappy about that because mine had been written in the suburban comic mode—Erma Bombeck x Letters to *Playboy*—and with the giggle ban it bombed. It didn't make it into the *All Fours* sex fantasy chapter either, though I wasn't expecting it to.

I had never been to Vegas before! Even at the airport I could feel the miasma of vice in the air. In the taxi, the driver boomed, "So where are you ladies going tonight?!" and waggled his eyebrows suggestively, to which we responded, "To a poetry reading," at which he was struck dumb.

Whenever I am in a pedestrian-free city, I feel dumb indeed, as if I've lost part of my brain. Everything is plotted in advance— the easy-on-and-easy-off driving experience, the excess of parking. The drive-throughs and the In-N-Outs. Smooth, no friction. No tension, agitation, affliction! It's by design. With all your needs anticipated, you become manipulable putty—lassid, flaccid, passive, facile. An easy mark. *Lassid* is probably not a word, but my spell-correct isn't correcting it, so I'm sticking with it. There ought to be an adjectival form of *lassitude*, don't you agree?

The mind is avid for friction. It needs irregularity; it responds to novelty, likes learning. It wants bad things to happen; it wants you to sit in traffic, go the wrong way, get off the true path, get lost. Everyone knows that when you get back you only talk about your travel disasters, not how you were ensorcelled by comfort.

Maybe because of this, I brought *Powers of Horror: An Essay on Abjection* by Julia Kristeva, which I am reading in between two oil-shellacked ladies deep in Colleen Hooverville. I got stuck in one of those reading-re-reading loops in the Oedipus Rex section, going around and around in my brain like a ball in a roulette wheel. In the play—the greatest masterpiece of Greek drama!— Oedipus seeks to free Thebes from corruption, turns his strength, intelligence, and resolve toward this end, and, of course, ultimately finds that the corruption is himself.

As I was leaving Las Vegas after my previous visit, I missed the turn onto the highway, and ended up in the part of Las Vegas that the Chamber of Commerce and the gods of Mammon don't want you to see. A place where the unhoused and addicted and impoverished people are, bent over and bruised from malnutrition, meth, violence. The people that the good times excluded, or were beached when the party ended.

It's not immediately clear how either the tourists robbed by the slot machines or I, with my pool-side drink and pretentious book, am responsible for these people being here, but we are. Take a few wrong turns on the highway of life and we're here, not at the Bellagio. We're not in traffic; we *are* traffic. Oedipus, c'est nous.

Another drink, please, pool guy!

I write to you from this dumb corner, McSweetie, a patsy for the gargantuan grift that is Las Vegas. I am not resisting. I subside into my poolside chaise. You'd think there was no suffering in the world. But I am weeping with-out the faintest idea of what I am weeping about. I have been led so far away from my terrors, and am so comfortable, I don't know why I am crying. Crying into my champagne, my coconut-scented sunscreen, my bottomless mai tai, my Coke Zero.

This place addles my brain. I am desperate to get back to San Francisco, but I can't move. Let's meet up when I recover. The sun is setting. The ice has melted into my drink. Don't forget me!

Love,

CATERINA FAKE
LAS VEGAS, NV

DEAR MCSWEENEY'S,

I rode a bike for the first time in years because a friend I was visit-ing in Germany wanted to bike to a lake. I used to bike regularly but stopped when I moved from the flat roads of the Midwest to the hills of San Francisco, and now I live in an apartment at the top of a hill that is painfully steep on both sides. My bike collects dust in the basement. If someone stole my San Francisco bike, which I've had for twelve years and have moved to eight different apartments, I prob-ably wouldn't notice.

On this trip to Germany, I rented a bike to get to the lake beach and rode behind my friend and her daughter, whose stuffed-animal dog peeked out from the side of her toddler seat. Even though my bike seat was at its lowest setting, I was still riding on tiptoe when seated, and the handlebars felt farther away than I would have liked, which reminded me of the time in college when I borrowed a friend's bike to get to the burrito place before it closed. He was at least a foot taller than I was, and he watched as I stood on a curb to get onto his bike. I pedaled away, unable to sit down.

I hadn't planned to go to a lake, so I hadn't packed a swimsuit. My friend asked if I would swim in my underwear, and I said that no one would be convinced that my underwear was a swimsuit. "Not even in Europe?" Not even in Europe. I didn't pack a swimsuit, even though later I'll be staying at a hotel with a pool, because I never enjoy swimming in hotel pools. They're oddly sized. Sometimes there are families with children splashing, and I don't want to disturb their fun with my pathetic attempt at a lap. Sometimes I prefer empty pools, but I'm unsettled by the echoes of my splashing and by the thought of dying alone in a pool and someone reviewing the security-camera footage to observe my watery death.

I only recently learned to swim. I suppose, technically, I relearned how to swim. When I was a child, my parents took me to swim lessons at the YMCA so I wouldn't drown immediately if I encountered water. I've spent most of my life dog-paddling nearly as well as my old dog, who was also capable of not drowning immediately as she paddled to shore with tiny paws. Thirty years after my first YMCA lessons, I signed up for adult swim lessons at the San Francisco Chinatown YMCA, where teenage boys taught me how to swim, and I never felt as close

to my own mortality as I did when they would solemnly answer my questions with the same respect they probably showed the aunties water-walking in the far lane.

I learned to swim well enough that I signed up for a gym membership and went swimming a few times a week. By my calculations, I would need to swim eleven times a month for the membership to feel worth it financially. Who cared about my health. Swimming at the gym always felt like a near-death experience even though I could touch the bottom of the pool. Sometimes I shared my lane with the water-walkers, who passed me in my slow crawl. Sometimes in the late afternoon, I would swim through sunbeams from the skylight, and I was enchanted by the rippling shadows on the bottom of the pool and didn't feel like I was going to die.

When I started to ballroom dance again and met a dance partner who wanted to take lessons, I stopped swimming because I couldn't afford a gym membership as well as dance lessons. I used to dance competitively when I lived in the Midwest, and when I started dancing again, my dance partner would lead me into moves that I did from muscle memory. I would be startled by the memories of dancing those same steps over a decade ago. Now I share the dance floor with people more than twice my age, who outdance me in energy and stamina. At competitions, I'll put on false eyelashes and a heavy rhinestone-encrusted dress to dance to ninety-second songs for a total of six minutes, and then walk off the dance floor to ungracefully hike up my skirts for air circulation. While I'm gasping for oxygen, senior citizens with perfect makeup and hair will glide by, song after song, with the most beautiful smiles.

In Germany, I waded into the lake with my friend's toddler, and at the bottom there were small, smooth pebbles glistening in the rippling shadows. The daughter reached down and placed a handful of these stones in my palm, and, while I wanted to keep the stones forever, when she turned her back to me, I dropped them back into the water.

SARA FAN
LEIPZIG, GERMANY

THE ORTS

by EMILY CROSSEN

TO SPEAK OF YOUR failures is pure vanity. For some time now, however, I haven't been able to stop talking about mine. And so it was out of exasperation, I suppose, that a friend recently suggested I try something new.

Everyone's doing autofiction, she said. It sells! Why not "mine the self," as she put it, for material? Isn't that where the truest vein lies, anyway? The deep gold seam?

At the time, I demurred. My friend is not a writer. (Is anyone?) But then I thought perhaps in fact it made her somewhat more of an authority than any writer could be. She reads books from time to time, and when she doesn't like them, she stops. There are no psychological impediments—which is to say, hang-ups—getting in the way of her good judgment.

Okay, I thought, I'll do it. I'll write about myself.

I started out full of hope:

I was born on an afternoon, in a city, in winter. It was raining or snowing: it was, let's say, precipitating. I had parents, and they were kind or cruel, attentive or indolent, good or not good, I guess, but I've never had any others so it's difficult to know which. I went to school. I did well there: I was exacting. Meanwhile, I was liked or hated or probably no one cared. I studied and graduated and cobbled together a "career." I married; I divorced; I married again. I had a daughter. When she was born, it was like a bomb went off, I love her so much.

But what happened most was time passed. I grew older— that much is indisputable. And through it all, under cover of nights, free in the secret hiding places, I ate what I would of trash, and was indistinguishable from it, trash, amongst which I move always unseen—

I stopped. It'd gone sideways. I shook my head to try to dislodge the dream, the possession. Then I began again:

Time passed, and time passed and passed, and I passed my life moving always unseen low to the earth, down by the damp earth, intelligent enough to make a small place there, yes, in the earth, underneath, we are snug with our small ones, we who eat especially the orts—

No, no, no. No no.

trash, we, running beneath warm pipes, alive to the world, alive to its every scent, its every drip and scrape, capable of fitting me in narrow gaps, fitting me into a city in which I fitted, in which I went without caring, no caring, not for other creatures, caring not, caring not a single jot—

Suddenly I saw; I understood. It was the other one writing: the one that hides. The one I've long referred to as "the ratself" in my private thoughts.

She, not I, would make a good subject for an autofiction. But I can't tell you about her, because there aren't "facts." In the span of memory, she's always been with me. Probably it's because of things that happened that she first appeared. I don't know. I only know she sometimes steers my outward life. That is, her will to solitude steers my outward life. I don't respond to emails; I can't see a friend unless I've tricked the ratself into it by many delays. Where do you go? my friends want to know. I can't say: Oh, back into my hole! This is the truth, though not one I can say. I suppose I could say it as a joke, but there's always the fear that no one will laugh and then I'll have to explain. Explain what? Explain that I am also a rodent.

She is cruel, the ratself. A tyrant. At times, however, I feel an almost convulsive gratitude for her. When I finally see a friend, my eyes fill with tears to think of this rodent's generosity and her cruelty—that she has let me out to see a friend. *She* taught me about generosity and cruelty: that they are twin exercises of the same power. And it's accurate to say "power," for I can't get around her or dispose of her. Imagine therapy!

Imagine lying on a couch, speaking of some original trauma! I'm not anxious or depressed; I'm a night-creeper, slick as a big turd.

But I have tried: I've tried to get rid of her. First, I endeavored to treat myself so well, with so much care and gentleness and light, that she would never emerge again. She likes darkness; she likes holes. If I were to come out aboveground into the sun? If I were to climb out and stare up at that cleansing, bleaching eye all day? To lie motionless at night on top of the dirt, exposed? She couldn't bear it. So I've tried luxuriating in baths and meditation and self-affirmations. I've tried believing in my own actions; I've tried praising my own creations. I've tried forgiving myself for every mistake; accepting every fault; making peace with every shortcoming; letting my husband love me; letting my daughter, my mother, my friends. Loving them back unreservedly and without apology. I have tried to live, in short, as I think others do. I even believed in this life. It's as real as the other. But it can't persist. As soon as the light goes out, her beady eye blinks open.

She's never gone. She's just hiding. Elusive—that's what she is. She doesn't look at herself willingly. If she finds herself in a mirror, she turns away. No use in vanity—we must credit her there. She steals back into the dark. She waits for the dark to come so that she may scurry out into it.

Does she kiss my husband? Hug my daughter? Think my thoughts? Is she there when I'm sleeping? If I lie in the sunshine with the tall grass at my ears, if I'm free and the clouds roll by and underneath the sky, someone embraces me, and that's all of time passing, for a moment, just warmth spreading between bodies—Is she there?

I have tried to talk to her. Who are you, where did you come from, why are you here, what do you want from me. Of course she can't answer. She doesn't come when summoned. I know her only from what appearances she deigns to make, and then her thoughts are muddled, subterranean, the tenses strange, she has her anxieties, of course, she has her fears, alive to it all, scents on the wind, the predators, the baits, the glue, the buckets, the poisons, the trap slapping in half the body suddenly slapped in half, the wheels rolling over her babies, the trash can out of which one cannot chew, there are such, there are traps, traps that cannot be chewed out of, even there where fetid fats call, where peach pit strings sweetly, where spill of grease lapped on plastic, birdcarcass whitecake papertowel strawberries, even there in sweetness traps, traps, she, I, who eats orts, who am trash, was trash, had to have been, wouldn't have been but for, would never have had to have been but for, but am, will be, was ever, as ever, trash, but still has, yes, in the dark, yes, heard the stories, within walls, within dark, where one at times hears the stories, next to the lives of those who speak, always next to that, there, where one hears them once heard while dinosaurs died, ugly mammals, we ugly mammals, in dirt survived, once heard that, take that home to the small ones I did, down in dirt, who eat orts, once also rhyme recited somewhere in darkness by those who speak, imagine, imagine those who speak speaking of bootless cries, bootless cries! for us who eats orts imagine, under dirt, whether heaven hears, heaven is not, heaven never was, hears, bootless, in any case, imagine—

When my friend and I next had lunch, I put my hand over her hand on the table and said: I love you, my friend, thank you for your good advice, despite my long absence I did appreciate it, and after all isn't it best, really, just to write the simple truth, just that, just that, to write, that is, what I know.

THE PILL

by SASHA GRAYBOSCH

LOUISE LIKED MANDY, AND Mandy liked Louise, but Mandy had been eating lunch with Peg since before Louise was hired, so if Louise wanted to eat lunch with Mandy, she also had to eat with Peg. Peg had led an interesting, challenging life, Mandy told Louise, but Louise hadn't heard much of it. So far, she knew Peg by her carefully portioned meals packed in mason jars and the set of anecdotes she deployed to illustrate this or that warning or theory or dubious maxim, like a country preacher.

The three women met at a picnic table on a grassy plot by the parking lot every day at noon, even though Peg complained about the exhaust when cars pulled in, and they had to wave hello to coworkers entering the building, like a professional greeting committee. It was either this or sit out front in the shade, and they all wanted the vitamin D.

Today Louise had tuna, Mandy had leftover shawarma, and Peg had celery sticks smeared with nut butter and goji berries. Peg was waving a log in the air as she urged Mandy to quit taking the pill.

"You should do it. You should get off it immediately," Peg said, as though hormonal birth control were a runaway train barreling in the wrong direction. "I felt like a completely different person when I quit." She spoke of the pill part of her life like a bad dream she didn't know she was having. Mood swings, migraines, swollen toes. It wasn't until she stopped taking it, to get pregnant with her son, that she discovered the root cause.

Mandy nodded as she chewed, her expression compliant but uncertain. She'd been feeling down and restless lately, she'd told them, her sex drive sputtering. She'd spent so much money on planner supplies from a Japanese stationery company—pens and stickers and washi tape and zippered pouches to store them in—it was like she'd been shopping in some kind of fugue. And none of it helped. Her future still looked like shit. Stopping the pill was at least something new to try.

Louise gently introduced the idea of counseling, but Peg kept tugging the conversation back to the pill.

"It messes with your head. It's tricking your body into thinking you're pregnant, for *forever*," Peg said, "and the doctors act like it's nothing. They give it to people for cramps and skin problems, but it doesn't *solve* them. It just puts the problems to sleep for a while, when it isn't waking new ones up." She pointed her celery stick at Mandy. "The pill is a mask. It's covering up who you really are."

Louise, sitting outside the celery's field of judgment, still bristled, unsettled by the implication that the last fifteen years of her own life on the pill had not been lived by her true self. This was why she didn't like eating with Peg. Another day, another way to end lunch feeling weird. Peg was one of these purity people, always going on about how things were done in caves, idealizing an unmedicated state while simultaneously mega-dosing plant powders. Louise attempted an interjection, but her indignation scattered her focus, and Peg had moved on to the increased risk of blood clots on the pill, which Louise could not dispute.

Peg finished lunch early—off to stretch, using the railing of the wheelchair-accessible ramp—and Louise pulled Mandy aside on their way in. "You know Peg's quite a bit older than we are. She probably took an earlier generation of the pill, before they worked out the hormones. Don't let her get to your head."

"It's okay," Mandy said, extracting her indoor cardigan from her tote. "I think it's what I needed to hear."

A month later, Mandy quit Lappsen Inc.

Louise had taken a long weekend to see family out of town

and returned to find an empty desk—Mandy's array of pastel highlighters and her scrunchie bowl and jumbo nut pack vanished, her workspace wiped clean. She'd left her succulent on Louise's desk with a little smiley-face note. *Don't water me*, the note said. *I'm not real.*

Gone.

Leaving Louise to eat with Peg.

"I have the scoop if you want to hear it," Peg said, blowing on a hot spoonful of squash soup. She was friends with Mandy on social media, a step Louise hadn't taken, preferring to keep her work and home lives separate. Mandy was using her savings on a solo cross-country RV trip, winding through the Midwest and camping for a week at the Grand Canyon. After, she was going to apply to law school, finally taking the plunge to start a career that mattered. She quit social media, too, after she posted the updates. "She seemed happy," Peg said.

Louise tried to square the image of the Mandy she knew—Mandy wearing her large noise-canceling headphones into the bathroom, Mandy struggling to open a pack of printer paper, Mandy organizing the employee pet photo wall on her own time, staying late to correct others' unattractive font choices—with the Mandy presently flying down a highway in a motorhome, on her way to cook beans under the stars. The Mandy who took financial planning courses at the library on the weekends was the same Mandy who woke up and said, *Screw it—enough of that?*

"It's just so sudden," Louise said.

"That's how it goes with the pill," Peg said. "She came back to herself."

"Did Mandy say that?"

"Just a hunch."

Louise caught the eyes of every passerby, hoping someone might take a seat and deflate the tension, change the topic, but there were no takers. "Do you ever think about quitting, Peg?" Louise said.

"Nah," Peg said. "I like making schedules. I like access to paper supplies. I'm good where I am." She was stirring seeds into a jar of green goop. "I've seen *way* worse. What about you? Everything okay in your world?"

Louise inflated, deflected, turned the focus around by asking about the goop.

Louise drove home that evening with a twist in her stomach. *Was* everything okay in her world? She slept badly most nights, disliked 30 percent of her body, and occasionally had fits of panic in which she understood that her entire life was an accident of circumstances, that none of it had been chosen by her as much as fallen into with lazy resignation, and she sensed with sorrow that somewhere, off in the intangible distance, another her was living her actual life, a bold life of action and exhilaration and surprise, with brunch and more friends and satisfying work, another city, another destiny. Maybe she was an artist, maybe she had kids, maybe she sold heirloom pumpkins at a farmers' market. Louise took Gas-X at least once a week; she had wiry hairs on her nipples; she felt turned on by her partner only occasionally, loving him as she would a worn-out teddy bear from childhood, preserving their bond out of loyalty and respect for the past. She chewed her fingernails to the quick and never *didn't* feel at least a little bit tired. She kept saying she wanted to learn another language, and never did.

But wasn't that just how it was, being human?

She tried to think back to the Louise she was before she started taking birth control—a girl of sixteen. Discovering sex, finding her powers, but a little idiot, too, and in many ways still a child. She'd been on the pill for so long that Louise didn't even know what real periods were like, or what it felt like to ovulate, or how she was without it, in general. On the one hand, so what? On the other hand, it was like hearing a knock on the door, a stranger on the other side, a person allegedly more *her* than she was.

Goddamn it, Peg, Louise thought, and switched off the engine: home.

The internet held forth. Articles and blogs shared cautions and urgings: Go off; Stay on, often in direct contradiction. If she stopped taking the pill, she might experience changes in weight, emotions, digestion, energy, skin, hair growth, and desires—some for the better, some for the worse. She might discover she was no longer attracted to her partner, if she'd met him on the pill, which she had. She looked over at him on the couch, twizzling his mustache, shopping for pants. "What?" he said.

Perhaps even her reproductive ambivalence would be unsettled by the change, a possibility she welcomed—a firm craving one way or another would at least relieve the drain of uncertainty, the paranoia of future regret. Her partner, unhelpfully, held tepid, compliant opinions. For now, contraception could take other forms.

With her refill unfilled, the last days of her pack bore down, pink disks disappearing from their silver foil pockets. Seven, then four, then one.

She told herself she wasn't afraid, though she half expected to wake in the middle of the night in front of the fridge, tearing into raw steak.

Days passed, then weeks.

She examined every passing thought, every wisp of feeling, watching for a transformation. The changes were subtle, if not indiscernible, which somehow made it worse. Was this grumpiness as she fished for the crummy kitchen sponge in the dishwater the last wheeze of the past, or the appearance of her true personality? What about this pimple, that bloat, this fatigue, that burst of fervor? She was really enjoying this clementine, a calm benevolence pervading her mood. Would she have felt this way on the pill? Would she have impulse-purchased the clementines on her way to the checkout line at all?

She took walks alone. She looked up at the stars. In her yard, she encountered a small, broad-leaved weed she thought she recognized as edible, and stuffed a handful of its leaves into her mouth. The act transmitted a thrill that seemed youthful and novel, unlike the next ten minutes, which she spent reviewing photos to confirm she'd ingested nothing toxic.

Another month went by. She asked her family and friends if they noticed anything different about her, but she didn't ask Peg. She hadn't told Peg a thing, even as they continued to eat together, awkwardly discussing office gossip and rising sea levels—a mutual interest—and avoiding any territory of conflict.

"You've been asking me more often what I notice about you," Louise's partner said. "That's the number one thing I notice." Perhaps even Louise's obsessive tracking was a new trait, meaning an old trait that had previously been masked by the pill. But then again, couldn't anything that changed you be a sort of mask? Exercise. Love. Living in Cincinnati versus Quebec. What part of oneself *wasn't* a mask—was there some irreducible, unalterable nub?

Time slipped Louise into a series of selves, as it does. She wanted. She ran errands. She pissed. She spoke. She ate toast. Was she there yet? When would it all settle in? Was she this thought and that mood, or that thought and this mood, or the spaces in between, when she forgot to look inside herself and ask?

*   *   *

Eventually, the pauses widened. Louise prevailed as Louise. No stifled urges came howling back, no radical personality changes, and no abrupt awakenings of clarity or energy, either. She rubbed her partner's tight shoulder muscles with begrudging affection. Eating breakfast, she imagined a toddler slapping the tabletop and deduced no new insight. She didn't feel like a completely different person. She felt like Louise, with less regular periods and a few more zits.

When Louise thought about the past, the pill part amid all the rest, she thought she saw subtle divisions, gradient shifts in tone, never changing quickly or all at once. It was impossible to say what caused what, what stopped or started when. The movements in her life gathered slowly, under the surface, culminating in wavelike succession.

In a way, Louise was disappointed with the results of her trial, but she felt smug knowing that Peg was wrong. Her foundation was sturdy; she'd been herself all along. Curiosity satisfied, she went back on the pill.

Peg never noticed anything, of course. She was busy explaining an elaborate envelope-stuffing savings method she'd discovered online, which involved withdrawing all your paychecks in cash and storing the bills in fancily labeled envelopes, thereby avoiding credit cards and stashing funds for big purchases. "It's important to really see your money," Peg said. "It's a powerful thing, to hold it and watch it grow in the right direction." She was saving for a trip to the Maldives. Louise didn't know why. She didn't ask.

*   *   *

The following winter, Peg had a stroke. It was her second, though the first one, years ago, had been minor—a "mini," as they're called—with effects lasting only a day.

Louise signed the cards and chipped in for flowers. She read the updates sent by the office leadership: brief, positive summaries of Peg's progress, collected through her son. Peg had stabilized in the hospital. She started outpatient care. She was "fighting her way back to full strength, conquering this challenge like so many others in her life," and couldn't wait to get back to the office. Her desk remained Peg—big binders, a compressed-air keyboard duster, a book on leaky-gut syndrome fringed with sticky notes, an ergonomic foam footrest tucked under the chair. Her money tree plant turned yellow and dropped its leaves from overzealous communal watering.

Louise ate alone in the usual place, reading articles on her phone, enjoying the silence. She felt a little guilty taking pleasure in the solitude, but she figured she might as well enjoy it. She knew it wouldn't last.

In the third month of Peg's absence, a notice went out that she was not quite 100 percent and was going to be out indefinitely. The company and the entire team at Lappsen wanted to thank Peg for her many years of service and wish her the very best in her recovery. It wasn't clear on whose side the decision was made, but one Monday morning, Peg's desk was clean.

Whenever Louise passed it on the way to the bathroom, she thought of Peg flexing the mesh back of her chair to stretch, rolling out her wrists; Peg's barking laugh echoing through the open office floor plan; Peg filling her personal teapot at the heated-water dispenser. Each day, Peg returned to Louise through the emptiness of the desk, a little daily dose.

"She didn't sleep well last night," the son told Louise, apologetic. "She was excited to see you, though." Peg sat grimacing in a ratty recliner, uncharacteristically hunched and largely unresponsive to Louise's nervous chatter. Peg looked tiny in a gray sweatshirt, and her hair—normally teased—fell flat against her skull. Her eyes held an obstinate tension, as though she were being held captive against her will.

Louise told Peg she'd started her own envelope savings fund, just one, for a new couch, and it did help to see the money in one place. She rambled about the office: Kerry was pregnant again, Tim moved to Arizona, the Lappsen intramural softball team beat Keinner's. "I don't want that," Peg said loudly, frowning. She settled into the chair and closed her eyes, either sleeping or taking herself away.

"For the most part, she's doing much better," the son said softly. He enumerated her accomplishments in motor control, her improved speech. There was this one weird thing that persisted, something he hadn't even known was possible—she could write, and she wrote a lot, but she couldn't read what she'd written.

The clock on the wall ticked. The son excused himself to lead Peg back to her room. When he touched her arm, she started and her eyes momentarily flailed open in fear.

"Mandy," Peg said, looking over her shoulder as they rounded the corner to the hallway, "you shouldn't let them change your hair."

A door swung open, water ran, shuffles. Louise assumed she should wait to say goodbye to the son. She put the box of dark chocolates she'd brought on the coffee table and slipped the card back into her purse. She'd written something regrettable about the future, the Maldives. She'd send another card. The son's house was chaotic—the unpleasant, electronic-centric mess of a young man, though he must have been in his thirties. Through a doorway to the kitchen, she glimpsed boxes of cereal and mac and cheese and bags of chips, noting that Peg must be flipping out over all the processed food, but then again, she wasn't sure. She stood to examine a series of cards lining the fireplace mantel and a framed picture of people in sunglasses on a boat. If Peg or the son was one of them, she couldn't tell. On a tray by the armchair, she looked down to see the top page of an open spiral-bound notebook— the kind they stocked at the office—each line covered with Peg's handwriting, at a slant. *This darkness*, Louise read, and looked away, before she could read any more.

*   *   *

Jodie was the new Peg. She sat across from Louise at the picnic table, stabbing a plastic fork around a bowl of chopped salad from the expensive salad place down the street. She asked if Louise knew their coworker Kevin's story, if he was single, and how long it would take for the first paycheck to come through payroll. Today Louise had tuna, and a yogurt sprinkled with seeds. She went around the side of the building, to where no windows faced, and looked out across the empty lot protected on all sides by fence. Scrubby bushes, stretches of dirt. The clouds passed quickly, and the distant traffic made a low roar like waves. On her way inside, she passed a sign detailing plans for a forthcoming building expansion. In the renderings, all the people looked busy and happy but strangely out of place, as if they'd been plucked from another world mid-sentence and dropped into this one, and hadn't yet realized they were there.

THE PANTRY

by MATTHEW ROHRER

MY WIFE WAS FIDDLING around with some stuff in the pantry while I was reading on the couch, and then she left, and minutes passed, many minutes, and then suddenly a bottle clinked, falling against something, somehow she had touched this bottle so gently, with such delicate care, that even in knocking it over it took several minutes to fall, falling so slowly, the whole time I sat there reading it was falling, falling, through silence, in absolute darkness, while she was already on to something else, handling whatever this next thing was so softly, and whatever it was I wished it was me.

MERLIN

by MATTHEW ROHRER

AND THEN MERLIN (*WHO?*) touched me with the tip of his
wand and all I could see around me were the children these
people had once been, these people straggling in off the hot
avenues to sit heavily on the subway, but when I turned to
Merlin to ask him how these people could stand it, having
once spun around on merry-go-rounds till they heaved, and
ridden bikes for hours at a time, how they could accept these
old bodies, he just smiled and dissolved into the air. And to
answer your question, he was a wizard who lived backwards
in time.

HELL IS A THOUSAND EYEBALLS

by ICARUS KOH

A WARM BREEZE WHISPERED through Yang's hair, and with it came the scent of mist rising from hot sand in the grey morning. The air before him shimmered, but not in the sense of a mirage, but rather because reality itself was wavering softly in that spot. Yang knew better than to look at the arrival, so he fixed his eyes politely on the wall to his left. There was a cheerful light blue poster about vision health, a little bland but it did the job. Or at least, it did until the ripples in reality grew more violent and the fabric of the universe ripped with a sound that felt like a screaming pinball ricocheting around Yang's brain, pinging off every wrinkle. The wall Yang was looking at warped into a melted-wax facsimile of itself, its properties intrinsically changed by coming into contact with the bulk of the creature that emerged from the tear. The air trembled, as something from a place where name and form were unnecessary had shifted in the physical realm, shaking atoms from their places.

"HELLO, I AM HERE FOR MY APPOINTMENT WITH THE OPTOMETRIST?" a many-layered cacophony of voices boomed.

Yang winced. It felt like cold needles stabbing through his skull. "Inside voice, please," he said, reflexively. To be fair, he was very used to babysitting his younger cousins.

"OH, SORRY," the angel said, its voice still a jarring jumble of sounds but at least now at a slightly lower volume, though it still grated across his bones. It was a little hard to focus on the shifting mass of ever-rotating wheels and wings dripping fire, but that wasn't Yang's job. He was more concerned with the multitude of eyes. Yang had gained renown as an optometrist who treated any patient, regardless of race, religion, species, or living status. Though vampires, zombies, ghosts, and the like were technically undead, they were very sensitive about being called such. They preferred the term *differently alive*. It was a rather diplomatic affair to treat all manner of patients, and treat them well, but Yang had done it. Was famous for it, even. Which was how today's guest had found him.

Cassiel, the Many-Winged Seraphim, They of the Wheels and Fire and Eyes. Of course, this description could apply to many other angels, but Cassiel had dominion over wind and sand, and thus the shifting sands of the desert followed them, which was a good identifier. Yang suppressed a groan as the miniature desert infiltrated his office. The tear in the fabric of reality sealed shut behind Cassiel with a sound like a zipper, and the great conglomeration of wings, wheels, and eyeballs floated in the middle of the room, unrepentantly dripping heavenly fire everywhere.

It was a good thing Yang had insured everything in his office. Everything. He'd learned that the hard way when he lost his windows to a young fairy's panic attack. How could he explain to the builders that, yes, there used to be windows there; no, he wasn't joking; no, he couldn't prove it, because who took pictures of windows, but he promised there *were* windows, could they please put them back?

Yang hadn't set out to cater exclusively to such a unique clientele. He had just started his practice, and he'd always had a strict nondiscrimination policy. So when a family of concerned werewolves showed up looking for a solution for their abysmally nearsighted child who could wear glasses just fine in human form but lost them whenever he turned into a were-puppy, tripping over every rock and branch in the forest, well, who was he to turn them down?

They tried doggles first—dog goggles—but the thing about children and were-puppies is that they both hate keeping their clothes on, which includes goggles. Then they floated the idea of werewolf contact lenses, but the child howled and cried and refused to have fingers anywhere near his eyeballs. Yang had then had to get in touch with his great-grandaunt Himiko-sama, who was technically more of a great-great-great-many-times-great-grandaunt, but it had been too many generations to keep count. Himiko-sama was an ancient witch who had ruled a queendom of women ages ago, but had now retired to travel the world with her wife, Yuri, and their many cats. The family rarely saw the matriarchs, but there were a few reliable ways to reach them.

Plenty of incense sticks and broken crystal-rose shards later, Himiko-sama and Yuri showed up on Yang's doorstep and enchanted him a pair of transforming glasses that never fell off, tossed him a priceless sixteenth-century imperial Chinese vase as a souvenir, as well as a book of spells, "so you can figure your own shit out, boy," before disappearing in a cloud of cherry blossoms.

Yang's parents, who had avoided every family reunion because his mum desperately wanted to forget her magical origins, were terribly unhappy. They'd tried their hardest to keep Yang away from that side of the family his entire life. Of course, they couldn't hide him forever, especially when said family had the ability to appear on your doorstep. So Yang had grown up spending summers with his aunt Hitsuji in the Himalayas, helping her raise her flock of magical sheep. It was considered a mostly acceptable compromise, as long as he never brought any of those bad habits back with him.

The werewolf family had been ecstatic about the doggles

that Yang had enchanted to both morph with their child's shape and stay on his person. Word spread. And soon, more and more unique clients were showing up at Yang's practice, until he became the optometrist to go to for extraordinary creatures. He found himself making use of the spell book and the forbidden summer lessons more and more often, until he could no longer deny his affinity for magic.

This was the first time he had ever treated a celestial being, however, and he was hoping he'd be up to snuff. There were a *lot* of eyeballs.

Yang pulled out his reinforced clipboard with the stack of intake forms and cleared his throat.

"Excuse me, Great Winged One—"

"CASSIEL IS FINE," the angel interrupted.

"Okay, yes, Cassiel. I have a few questions for you before we can begin your checkup. First: Do you have a family history of eye problems?"

"I HAVE NEITHER A FAMILY NOR A HISTORY, FOR I AM AT ONCE IMMEDIATE AND INFINITE."

Yang looked at the list, which included questions like "Do you have any known allergies to medications, food, or other substances?" and "Do you or does anyone in your family have a history of diabetes, high blood pressure, heart disease, or any other health issues that can affect the whole body?," and crossed most of the questions out.

"Let's try this. I'm going to hold a pen before your eyes. Follow the movement as best you can."

"WHICH EYE?"

"I, um. We'll start with the one at the very bottom tip of your lowest left wing—no, no, left on my side—and work up. How about that?"

The incomprehensible mass of wheels and wings—all on fire, mind you—bobbed obligingly closer to Yang and extended the tip of said wing. The eyeball on that tip peered at Yang and winked. Or blinked. It was hard to tell when the eyes didn't come in pairs.

An eternity of eyeballs later, Yang's back was aching from all the contortions he had put his body through. His skin prickled uncomfortably from exposure to the constantly dripping heavenly fire. What was the point of having an eye on the inner rim of the wheel? What was that eyeball even looking at? Other eyeballs? He refused to believe that any creature on Earth needed that many eyeballs. Think of how fractionated their vision must be! But of course, Cassiel wasn't a creature on Earth. Who knows, maybe in the heavenly realm there was a great need to observe everything around you from a thousand different angles at once. Maybe heaven's residents rejoiced so much in being able to behold its splendor that they decided they needed to behold it over and over and over again, for all of time. Or maybe heaven didn't look like anything, and could be experienced only as a sensation fizzing on the ends of your neurons.

Yang didn't know what the afterlife was like, because the ghosts he had treated were mere echoes that had clung to the material realm. That's not to say they weren't *people*. They were as sentient as when they'd been alive. But ghosts could never change, never progress; they were fixed in a moment of time, suspended like a snapshot of a bird in flight. It was a bit like treating someone with dementia. They forgot the present, lost wandering through memories where their lives had once been bright.

Also there was the added complication of the undead— sorry, differently alive—like vampires, that were considered unholy. Not to mention the gay vampires, which was pretty much all of them. Yang had heard that the Christian God wasn't big on the undead, or gays, but they both still existed and were perfectly nice people, so he wasn't sure heaven was all that great. It was hard to stick to one religion when you had all sorts of supernatural creatures traipsing in and out of your office with the *worst* eyesight. Seriously. How on Earth had the Cyclopes managed to build a reputation for being fearsome cannibals when they had absolutely zero depth perception?

Bottom line: He wasn't in awe of heaven or God or, by extension, the angels, so this patient's visit wasn't, like, the experience of a lifetime or anything. It was just an immense pain. Somewhat literally.

"Let's take a break now, okay, Cassiel? Now that we're done with the eye-muscle test, we're gonna move on to the visual acuity test. Don't worry; I'm just going to ask you to read some letters off a chart. I'm mortal, though, and I need some rest. You don't mind, do you? I blocked out the whole day for your appointment," Yang said.

The angel bobbed up and down in what Yang assumed was an approximation of a nod. Or a shrug.

"THE LORD SET ASIDE THE SEVENTH DAY FOR REST. FOR REST IS GOOD, AND REST IS HOLY."

"Oooookay, then," said Yang, and he settled himself on a chair. "So, what do you do for fun?" He felt obligated to make some sort of small talk with his patient.

"FUN?"

"Oh, um, like hobbies? Free time?"

"TIME IS A MORTAL CONCEPT. AS IS FREEDOM. I DO NOT KNOW WHAT THESE HOBBIES YOU SPEAK OF ARE, HOWEVER."

"Oh! Like. Um. Things you do to relax. For no reason except that you like it." A small thunderclap shook the room as every single eye on the angel blinked simultaneously.

"I SUPPOSE I ENJOY PLAYING *MINECRAFT*."

Yang stared at the seraphim. The seraphim STARED BACK.

"*Minecraft*. Like. The game with blocks."

"YES. IT IS, AS YOU SAY, FUN."

Yang opened his mouth to respond, couldn't find any words, closed it, then half thought about the possibility of Wi-Fi in heaven. That led to a rabbit hole of social media for angels, computers in heaven, how do they use computers with no hands are there angel engineers are there angel computer scientists oh my GOD THERE ARE GAMER ANGELS CAN THEY PLAY ON OUR SERVERS TOO and then he shut down that train of thought before his brain imploded in a burst of bloody matter.

"Oh, brilliant!" he chirped brightly. "What do you like most about it?"

There was no significant change in the angel's demeanor, but he swore they perked up a little.

"CREATION. THOUGH I AM BUT GOD'S SERVANT, I, TOO, CAN PLAY MY PART IN WEAVING THE WORLDSONG. ALSO, THE ANIMALS ARE CUBES. IT IS... CUTE."

"Cute. Right. Yeah, I think they're cute too."

The two of them lapsed back into silence, but Yang fancied it was a fraction more companionable now.

It was *difficult*, to say the least, to get Cassiel in the right configuration to read off the alphabet charts. Turned out the wheels constantly rotated, and no, it wasn't voluntary, so Cassiel couldn't control the rotation enough to stop for long enough to look at a goddamn chart. God*damn*, indeed. Yang had never been sold on the idea of an almighty god, and now he definitely wasn't. Who the fuck designed creatures like these? It was as if when God was making the angels, he'd stuck his hand deep into a jar of googly eyes and pulled out a fistful, then thrown them on top of an unfinished car masquerading as a plane.

Did God have something against optometrists in particular? Who needed this many eyeballs? AND WHY WERE ALL OF THEM DEFECTIVE IN SOME WAY?! He'd barely gotten through half of them, but already he could tell that most needed some kind of prescription, and the kicker was that none were the same. It was always some complicated thingamadoodad like an eyeball with astigmatism combined with long-sightedness, right next to a wildly shortsighted eyeball. How the fuck was he supposed to deal with that?

He thought about giving up. Calling it quits. Sure, he'd had a reputation for fulfilling each customer's request for the past twenty years, but every man meets his match at some point, and this might just have been it. He could see it now. He'd drop his clipboard onto the melted floor and shrug.

Sorry, Cassiel, but I can't do this. You'll have to find someone else, he'd say.

BUT THERE IS NO ONE ELSE, Cassiel would cry.

Well then, good luck with an eternity of bad eyesight, Yang would reply nonchalantly, and sweep out the door.

Oh, the consequences would be horrendous. The Zocdoc review. The one-star rating. The hit to his reputation. His employees would be so confused when they came in the next day (Yang had given them all the day off to deal with The Client himself). But none of that mattered if Yang intended to disappear. Aunt Hitsuji would take him in. She'd talked about leaving the sheep farm to him before. He'd just inherit it a bit sooner than expected.

A slightly more pressing concern was the thought that refusing service to one of God's messengers might turn all of heaven against him, colossally fucking up his afterlife, but Yang *really* didn't care. He wasn't Christian anyway. Who was he to say that that particular afterlife was going to be his? Besides, it wasn't like he had been a shoo-in for heaven before this appointment.

He didn't think he'd lived a particularly remarkable life. Sure, he'd helped a bunch of people, but it had been for profit. He had to pay off his mortgage, after all. The world of the fantastical could be annoyingly mundane. There was even an Immigration Agency for the Fae Wilds now! Something about too many undocumented changelings that deserved their own rights. It wasn't politically correct to just spirit a human away nowadays; you had to go through the proper channels. All this to say, Yang was seriously considering calling it quits.

He took a deep breath and tried going to his happy place. He thought of the mists on the lake, the cool air on his cheek, watercolor-orange sunlight blurring through the fog as the birds called to one another in the morning. He could smell the aquatic greenness of the water, hear the gentle rushing of the waves lapping against the shore. He curled his fingers into the wool of a Hitsuji sheep. It was thick and soft, like sinking through dreams.

A family of ducks honked softly as they nosed through algae for breakfast. Warm sand shifted underfoot. He sighed and dug his toes into the sand. He encountered the harsh reality of shoes instead. Those leather shoes that had cost way too much of his paycheck, but his best friend had assured him that they'd help him look like the professional doctor he was instead of a scruffy, wide-eyed student.

Yang supposed it had worked, because here he was standing in the same room as the most illustrious client he would ever have, unless God himself decided he needed an eye checkup. There was no lake. There were no bird calls. There was *too much fucking sand*.

He could feel it rubbing against his ankles, squirming sinisterly into his socks. The socks he cherished because they were made of merino wool sheared from the magical sheep that Aunt Hitsuji raised, and enchanted to be extremely fucking comfortable. They were always precisely the right temperature and never made him sweat.

Yang had always been ambivalent about the beach, but at that moment he decided that he really, REALLY hated sand.

"EYE DOCTOR. ARE YOU LOST?"

Lost in your fucking multitude of defective fucking eyes, he thought bitterly. God, what he'd give to just... not be here. He had a protective shield cast over his office but it still hurt to be in such an otherworldly creature's presence, and he felt like his organs might bleed.

Instead, he pasted a plastic smile on his face and replied,

"Just a little distracted for a second. You know how mortal brains are. Okay, I've just about gotten all your prescriptions, so how about we discuss options for frames. Feel free to browse the shelves outside."

And then, with a tiny flash of hope igniting in his soul, he chirped, "Or even contacts! Have you ever thought about contacts?"

For the first time in a while, he prayed. Please, God, Zeus, Buddha, whoever, just please let Cassiel choose contacts. It would make his life so much easier. Instead of suffering Cassiel's presence while they dithered about choosing frames, Yang could dismiss them now and order the contacts, then deal with the torture of trying to teach a fingerless creature how to apply contact lenses to all one thousand of its eyeballs at a later date. A much, much later date.

Please. I'll do anything. I'll convert to Christianity for the rest of my life. I'll make daily offerings of freshly slaughtered lambs. If that's too old-school, I'll donate some cryptocurrency in your name and light a candle. Just a little crumb of mercy. The tiniest, most minuscule crumb of mercy. Come on, God, aren't you all about mercy? Live, laugh, love, forgive and forget, and all that. Please. Give me a little something. Anything, he thought.

His lifetime of agnosticism came back to bite him in the ass, as Cassiel tilted to the side a little and asked, "CAN I GET BOTH?"

* * *

Some people prided themselves on not being quitters. They were the type of people who waded through a blizzard to get to school, while Yang was the kind of person who looked out the window, saw that it was snowing heavily, and rolled over and went back to sleep. These were the same people who either went on to discover a new strain of bacteria or burned out young and bright from the furious pace they set for themselves.

It wasn't that he lacked drive. He'd finished medical school. He just didn't believe in putting himself through more discomfort than was necessary to achieve his goals. It had been working pretty well for him thus far.

Which was why, as Cassiel browsed the shelves of frames in the shop outside, Yang packed his briefcase and made to climb out the window. Nothing was worth this amount of damage to his health—both mental and physical. He quit. Gave up. Done. It was over. Mortal bodies just weren't made to withstand the presence of a biblical angel for long. Fuck the protective shield; it wasn't doing shit. He could jump out the window and ask the wind to carry him away to Aunt Hitsuji. She lived on a mountain, in an idyllic cabin overgrown with flowers that bloomed all over its roof regardless of the season. She wouldn't mind. It would be like old times. An eternal summer. It had been forever since he'd had a vacation anyway.

"EYE DOCTOR. MAY I HAVE YOUR OPINION ON THIS STYLE?" Cassiel caught him with one leg out the window, briefcase in hand.

Yang wavered. He could just… not answer. He could already feel the wind tugging at his clothes, wanting to take him away from here.

"EYE DOCTOR? DOES THIS LOOK ALL RIGHT ON ME? I DO NOT KNOW IF PINK IS MY COLOR," Cassiel said bashfully, peeking through the doorway. "YOUR OPINION IS VALUABLE TO ME."

Swallowing a sob, Yang dropped his briefcase onto his office floor and pulled himself back into the room. The wind lifted the ends of his hair before letting go, disappointed that it couldn't sweep him into the sky.

He turned and looked at the angel hovering in his doorway. They were covered in an explosion of colors, all sorts of frames wedged onto their wheels and wings. The ones they were asking his opinion on were an outrageously bright neon pink with flamingo heads holding the lenses in place, perched on a pair of eyeballs in the middle of a wheel.

He hadn't thought anyone could possibly look good in those frames, but the effect of so many mismatched styles and colors all over Cassiel's incomprehensible body had the effect of making them look more approachable. *Cute*, even.

"They look great on you, Cassiel. Excellent choice. Anything else I can help you with?" Yang said through gritted teeth.

Time meant nothing anymore. He had been sinking for centuries. The stars careened overhead, trapped in their endless dance through the cosmos. Inhale: ash; exhale: dust. Yang had never been so aware of his meaningless flesh. When one spends one's entire day/year/lifetime in the presence of a creature that defies all bounds of mortality, one becomes rather disenchanted with one's own humanity.

He had thought that his lifetime of exposure to supernatural creatures and the shield cast over his office could numb him to the sheer weight of an angelic entity's existence, but there is a stark difference between a creature that walks the same dimension, no matter how inhuman, and one that was never meant to. There were probably no mortal magics that could truly negate the incompatibility between their existences. There was a reason that, historically, prior encounters with God's messengers were all prefaced with the statement "FEAR NOT."

Yang sent Cassiel to wait in the mostly destroyed waiting room while (supposedly) he filled Cassiel's orders on the computer in the back room. Instead, Yang was feverishly flipping through a large tome bound in cracked, stained leather. It had been sealed with duct tape and buried at the back of his bookcase full of reference texts, both magical and non-magical. The book's pages creaked instead of rustled when they were turned, like an old man's joints complaining. It emanated a musty warmth ripe with fungus rot, the stench of layers of decomposing leaf litter. Peeking through the remnants of destroyed duct tape was the title: *How to Reject Life and Accept Decay: From Mycelium to Demonic Rituals*.

The reason for Yang's abrupt conversion to radical nihilism was very simple: He was not a strong man. He had become the go-to optometrist for the supernatural world because (a) it was a niche no one else had filled and thus it ensured job security, and (b) he vaguely wanted to prove his immediate family wrong about magic. This job was proof of his success. His mother had been so afraid he would amount to nothing if he took after his matrilineal family.

"You need to get a nice, stable job in an ordinary field," she had said often throughout his childhood. "Something practical, like a doctor. Or an engineer. Nothing frivolous."

"Aunt Hitsuji says she needs someone to take over her farm, and I like the sheep. Can't I go do that? That's practical, isn't it?" little Yang had said, still bright-eyed and hopeful.

"Practical! Sheep farming! 神经病! Anata, can you believe what our son is saying? Where did we go wrong with this child?" she cried to her husband, who was a modest businessman with no loftier dreams than having his own corner office one day.

Yang didn't understand what was so impractical about sheep or farming, but he resolved to never bring it up again. He would go to a respectable university and enter a useful career, so he never had to see his mother look at him like that ever again.

Now here he was, with his ultimate patient. His life was a series of coincidences, and even his greatest rebellion was simply born of chance. He had to agree that despite the joy that fizzled through him whenever he found a solution for another unconventional client, he would not have the lingering shards of his sanity slipping slowly out of reach if he had gone for something like accounting.

He didn't really have a plan, besides the screaming thought that he had to get as far away from Cassiel as possible, no matter how polite they were. Being in the same room with the seraphim felt like being trapped in a fishbowl while getting lanced by lightning from all sides. It had been mildly irritating at first, no worse than a singular ant bite, but increased exposure had elevated it to the point that he felt a deep ache in his bones, and his organs trembled. His brain's feeble struggle to translate Cassiel's voice into interpretable speech that his mind could comprehend left him stretched, scraped, like butter over too much bread.

Various organic creatures have different coping mechanisms when confronted with an insidious foreign body that gets under their skin. Oysters grow pearls around irritants in their flesh. Something primal deep within Yang's brain gibbered frantically, seeking an escape to a place where no angel would ever trespass.

Each word Yang forced out vibrated his teeth unpleasantly, reminding him of the precarity of his bones. He was nothing more than meat clumsily slopping his way through the third dimension, meat held together by stringier meat that had gained the audacity of sentience by wrapping itself in a web of bioelectricity. This hypocritical meat sack was made of the same stuff as that which it considered prey, barely a blink away from returning to oblivion. He craved the void before creation. He had to return to non-sentience.

"EYE DOCTOR? ARE YOU LOST?" that accursed cacophony boomed. Describing Cassiel's communication as a "voice" was generous, as no voices on Earth echoed wetly within Yang's eyeballs.

Just a little longer. The portal to hell was almost complete. Soon, he could dive right through and let the flames of damnation wash away all consciousness.

Yang watched the unholy gash in reality shudder farther along its length, widening the wound between worlds. A cold light began to leak forth.

Then it closed.

"SILLY MORTAL, THAT IS THE WRONG DIMENSION. HOW COURTEOUS OF YOU, BUT I CAN FIND MY WAY HOME," the great seraphim chortled. "THIS CONCEPT OF 'CUSTOMER SERVICE' IS INDEED WONDERFUL."

Yang stared at the air before him that had sealed so neatly, erasing his ticket to paradise. He was startled into a semblance of coherence when he felt himself get picked up by *something* that his mind recoiled at, his senses screaming at one another to avoid conveying such sensation.

"COME, EYE DOCTOR. AS A REWARD FOR YOUR FAITHFUL SERVICE, I WILL SHOW YOU HEAVEN. I SIMPLY MUST RECOMMEND YOU TO ALL OF MY FRIENDS."

A tug and a gasp, and reality shattered into a thousand smithereens. Yang's last sensation was of being plunged into the heart of the sun, before his mortal soul splintered from the stress.

Cassiel's wail echoed through at least four dimensions, despairing at yet another attempt at correcting their vision gone awry.

"What did I tell the boy? Don't mess with things beyond your means. And now look at what he's done to himself. It's that silly girl, Yagi. She didn't bring him up right. Filled his head with nonsense. She should never have married that Chinese man."

"Himiko-koi, you can't say that anymore."

"Aiya, I don't care that he's Chinese, Yuri. He's a *man*. And a particularly useless one at that. Little Yang would have been educated properly if he'd been raised by women. Oh, my useless grandnephew. If only you had summoned us earlier, we would have guided you away from disaster…"

The matriarchs of the family gazed somberly at the warped ruins of Yang's office. They had left their exploration of the fairy chimneys of Cappadocia in a rush when Himiko's spell book had reappeared before her, something that should have happened only if she'd called it back, or if the current holder had been… incapacitated beyond recovery.

"He should've had better sense than to accept a visit from a *tenshi*, though. He knows enough," Yuri said, sweeping her foot through a mound of glittering sand.

"Men and their pride," Himiko muttered, shaking her head.

She reached for her wife and they dissipated in a swirl of pale pink petals that were swept into the sky by the eager wind.

PLAYSPACE

by CLARE BEAMS

WE, THE PARENTS, MOSTLY the mothers, had been coming to the Playspace for a long time. To this single large room with shelves of toys lining its walls we brought ourselves and our children every Tuesday and Thursday morning, or every Wednesday afternoon—whatever structure worked for and held up our weeks—to sit in the empty space in the middle while our children ran around taking toys off shelves and scattering them on the floor, or screaming when other children ripped them away, or just letting the other children take them, or turning, right before our eyes, into the children who took them from other children. All these actions equally, though differently, concerning. Within the Playspace's cushiony, diapery room, we marinated together in concern.

The day of the voice, we found that the empty space we were used to filling in this way had changed its shape while it waited for us. We stopped on the threshold and stared, bewildered, at the sunken amphitheater that had taken the place of the emptiness—or that cupped that emptiness, underscored it. An area become an arena.

Come in, please.

We flinched so hard our children felt it in our hands and hips and looked curiously at our faces. The voice seemed to come from the walls, making them all hum, as if the space had turned into a giant voice box.

"Is this a joke?" said humorless Beatrice.

Come in. Take a seat, mothers and/or parents.

Play, children.

All the toys you know are still here.

Every toy you could want—isn't that true?

Show me which toys you want.

Each of you, please, show me.

My daughter's wants were particular and unpredictable. She had been, in this space, six months old and one year old and two years old, and now she was two years and ten months old, and at none of those ages had she wanted anything I'd managed to foresee. She was not friendly. Since her infancy, in grocery stores and libraries, in this very Playspace, mothers and fathers, nannies and grandparents put their faces in her face to try to extract a smile, as if she owed them one.

This is not your face. Get out of it, my daughter's face said.

"She's not very happy, is she!" they sometimes remarked. As a habitual smiler, I found the dynamic terrible—I who had always given to anyone what they thought they were owed. I smiled extra-large in atonement, said, "Sorry!" I was parenting a child for whose admirable traits I couldn't stop apologizing.

A person had to work very hard for my daughter's smile, but when it came—there is no other way to say this—it was like sunshine.

Beatrice, the voice said now.

Beatrice startled. She and I referred to each other as *friends* because there wasn't a better word, but we didn't like each other. Her son, Charlie, was a genius. She would actually come right out and tell you this, in a stagy, thrilled whisper.

Charlie was three years old now and on the cusp of reading, Beatrice had told me yesterday. "How can you tell?" I asked.

"Look how he's looking at the words on those pages. You can tell he's really *seeing* them."

I was distracted into laughing because my daughter was eyeing a doll in a smaller girl's hands, readying her pounce/lunge.

"What's funny?" Beatrice said, her face alert in a new way, as if wondering where best to direct a bite.

That was the expression on her face now too.

Beatrice, please bring Charlie to the well.

"To where?"

But we all saw that the voice could mean only one place, given the place that had just appeared.

Beatrice looked at the rest of us, suddenly pleased, and gave a little shrug. Beatrice had always waited for someone to ask her to come to the center of things. She scooped Charlie up and walked with him down the one, two, three, four, five giant steps of the amphitheater, to its sunken floor. She had to take two steps of her own on each of the well's steps. In the middle she put Charlie down. He held her leg, blinking.

Sit down, Beatrice. All of you others too.

We were nervous. But we were also, as always, very tired, which made us do what we were told most of the time. We sat on the carpeted steps, higher up, and pulled our children into our laps.

Charles Leon Faber.

"How do you know his name?" said Beatrice.

On my lap, my daughter shifted. Her hot palm pressed my bare leg, and my skin beneath it sweated in a way that made me think of a footprint in snow.

CHARLES LEON FABER, the voice said, louder, *will bounce like a ball through his life.*

Beatrice's brow furrowed.

And here came the ball. Red rubber, duckpin-bowling size, rolling and, yes, bouncing down the stairs, one two three four five—one bounce per step—all the way to the bottom.

It rolled and then stopped against Charlie's shin, like a pet.

"Who threw that?" Beatrice said.

No one threw the ball, Beatrice. And everyone did.

"What? And what does that mean, he'll bounce like a ball?"

CHARLES LEON FABER will bounce like a ball through his life: a nice, round, soft, red ball, like this one.

I found I understood in a whole and visual way. I saw a ruddy-cheeked, round-faced adult Charlie buying a car, buying a house, going to work, going home, going on vacation with a constant rubbery smile on his face. I saw everything down to the way his hair would recede, pulling back like a gentle sea on his orb of a head. It would leave a pattern like the one on my daughter's head when her newborn hair had fallen out, that dark hair she'd had after birth and that had rubbed off, finely, all over her baby sheets, so she looked like a little balding man.

Like the balding man Charlie would become.

Were we all understanding in the same way? We were all seeing something—the mothers, anyway, if not the children: that was clear from the faraway expressions we wore.

This ball is Charles Leon Faber's now.

At first I heard, *This ball* is *Charles Leon Faber.*

"Nothing at the Playspace," said one of the mothers faintly, "belongs to any one child."

This ball does, now.

Charlie held his ball. Beatrice stood, picked Charlie up, and held him.

Clear the center, the voice said.

And so Beatrice did, climbing back up the wide steps, Charlie in her arms and the ball in his.

At home that night, after my daughter was asleep, I asked my husband, "What's the strangest thing that's ever happened to you?"

"What do you mean?" he said. He was looking at his computer and only partly listening. He played several different games that all looked similar to me: walls of scrolling text on black backgrounds.

I thought about the voice and Charlie, and then two-year-old Emma Shaler, who'd gone next and had been given a pointy-faced plastic horse figurine—*EMMA ROSE SHALER will turn a stalwart eye on all her years*—and then three-year-old Josey Printz, who'd been given a set of paints—*JOSEPHINE LILY PRINTZ will celebrate a formless freedom*. The way each mother's face was stripped naked when the gift was given, though the children just picked the toys up like they belonged in their hands.

It had been more unsettling seeing the horse and paints tumble down the steps, making their hard sounds (the thunk of the horse, the clatter of the paints), muffled only a little by the thin industrial carpet, than seeing the ball bounce. Watching, you couldn't help but understand that the world must have tilted to make them fall that way.

Three per day, the voice had said. *Like meals.*

We'd winced.

"Just a mystery, you know," I told my husband now. "Just something that didn't fit with what you thought you knew about the world."

"I don't think I know very much," my husband said, which was true: not that he didn't know much—he knew more than most people—but that he approached his surroundings with questions. Despite the computer, he would be likelier than most to listen to what I would say, if I were to proceed to really tell him. Likelier to help me think it through and understand what I should do next.

"Fair enough," I said, though it wasn't, really; I'd asked him to offer something and he hadn't. I could, of course, have pushed, or offered what I had. But what if I did that, explained everything, and he didn't understand, didn't want me to bring our daughter back there?

Because while I was afraid, I was also desperate to return. What if he couldn't see that I had this chance, this one chance, to know what our daughter would be given? What could any mother want more?

Back in the Playspace the next morning, Beatrice and Charlie weren't there, or Emma and her mother, or Josey and hers. "We think they're okay, though?" I said to one of the other mothers.

"How should I know?" she said. She looked like she'd been crying: her nose was red and running. She smoothed back her hair.

I imagined Charlie bouncing, not figuratively, off the walls of his house and into his mother—bruising her shins, hips, and stomach, as carrying him must have done from the inside. I imagined Emma angling her sharp face into her mother's and saying, *No, I'm not going*; Josey busily painting her hands and then putting them everywhere, touching everything in her house to lay claim.

Good morning, the voice said.

I jumped. Many of us did.

Gather, please.

My daughter took an instinctive step. I hated the sight of her walking thoughtlessly forward. It seemed so unlike her.

What if this voice was changing them before it ever told us who they were?

Terror seized me in its large cold fist and made me seize my daughter in turn: I gripped her hand tighter, then tugged. "Come on over here," I said brightly.

"What are you doing?" said the mother I'd been talking to before.

What I was doing: changing my mind. "We're just going to go play instead."

I pulled my daughter over to the bins of dollhouse people she liked so much that she often tried to hoard them behind her, like a jealous dragon guarding its eggs. I took them out, a mouthwatering array of her favorites—she seemed always on the verge of devouring what was most precious. The girl with the pink bow and the bendy legs, the mother with the long hair that my daughter liked to comb her fingers through. "Look, they can all be for you right now," I told her. "No sharing!"

Gather, please, all of you, the voice said.

"It says come," my daughter said.

"We're just doing our own thing." I picked up the mother and swished her hair through the air between us like a streamer. I bent the daughter's bendy arms around the mother's waist. "They love each other," I said. I knew everyone was watching and listening to me, and I wished, even now, that I could think of something cleverer for this mother and daughter to be doing. As a mother I was awful at playing. Awful at doing so many of the things I remembered loving to do as a child.

It's not time for other toys right now.

I looked up at the ceiling, trying to discern where it was watching from, speaking from. Had this ceiling always been so high? If the room had been full of water, I would have been hopelessly drowning down here.

A touch made me balk. My daughter closed her hand gently over mine, which was still closed over the mother doll. She looked at me a little warmly, a little sternly, the same look I'd used to tell her to stop grabbing and start taking turns, to become like other, more agreeable children.

What could I do but follow her?

My daughter did not get her turn that day. Maybe that was my punishment. We watched *PATRICK NATHAN ELLISON* receive a train—the metal blows of it on the steps like a crucial part falling again and again off some machine—and *SARAH LOUISA PETERS* receive a set of building blocks, and *MARSHALL SIMON*, who had, it seemed, no middle name, receive a stuffed elephant wearing a little pink shirt. References were made to *softness*, to *solidity that can be quantified*, and to *intrepid speed*. My daughter picked up the doll family, when the three turns were over, to play, more quietly than usual, until it was time to go.

Driving home, I vowed never to return, not ever.

My husband sighed that night when I dropped and broke a bowl while cleaning up after dinner. I burst immediately into tears.

"What is it?" he said, taking my wrist.

Our daughter was asleep upstairs. I was glad at least that she wasn't witnessing this, the end of the road of obedience, a place where any gentle reprimand was crushed because of the weight of all the effort that had come before.

"I'm teaching her all the wrong things," I said.

Not a lie, even if it wasn't the truth.

"What wrong things?"

"I keep telling her to share, and listen, and be nice. Why do I do that? Won't she just end up the one holding nothing?"

"Do you feel like you're holding nothing?"

He said this lightly, but it landed heavily, and we both

stared at it, sitting there between us, the question of my degree of emptiness.

Of course I did, some days. Cold winter mornings when I woke up and felt more exhausted than I had ever imagined a person could feel, more exhausted than when I'd gone to bed, and when my husband went to work and our daughter became my daughter and she and I were home all day with only each other. She wasn't nothing, he wasn't nothing—but sometimes the self they needed from me bore no real resemblance to who I actually was, so that I, the real I, was nothing, or might as well have been. And nothing couldn't hold them. Had no hands no eyes no ears no arms to do the holding with. Did it matter on what side the lack was, if the holding couldn't be done?

"Of course not," I said. What else was there to say, if we were going to continue?

When my daughter woke the next morning, I told her we were going to the zoo. This was her magical place, only for special occasions. She usually asked about it in the same wistful tone she used when asking if someday she could be a mermaid.

But she shook her head. "I want my toy."

I thought sometimes about what I would do if my daughter were to turn to me and say, *Mama, I want a strip of your skin.* I wouldn't, of course, run to the kitchen and grab a knife to undertake the detachment (from the forearm, maybe, or the stomach she'd left so squishy and stretched there was no way its skin would ever lie flat again). But the main reason I wouldn't do it had nothing to do with unwillingness. That could have been surmounted. The more important feeling I had was that it would be bad for her, to make a demand like this and have it obeyed—it would hurt her, damage her. I would be saying no, even to this, for her. Not because I was some extraordinary mother, but out of the instinct that makes a person swim toward the surface to breathe. An animal impulse, maybe not so much the surmounting of selfishness as the slight extension of it, the revision of the definition of *self*.

"The voice scares me, honey," I said to her.

She came closer and patted my arm. The expression on her face was like the sunshine smile in its preciousness, though what it expressed was pain at my pain.

"I want my toy," she repeated, and patted again the same strip of skin from my hypothetical slicing.

At the Playspace, my daughter and I sat on our step and blood throbbed in my throat while the voice bestowed a Barbie and a truck on, respectively, *THOMAS ROBERT HARRISON* and *ALASTAIR LUCAS STEVENS*. For *the smooth shape of an inner self*, and for *a friendly forward motion*.

We waited. The silence had an underwater sound in my ears and my daughter watched my face.

RUBY ELIZABETH SANDERS.

My daughter's name. It lingered and rang ceremonially. It's rare that you get to hear your child's full name that way. I remembered lying in the dark, with my hands on the swell of her inside my stomach, and whispering it, after my husband was asleep. *Ruby Elizabeth Sanders.* Just to make sure.

She held my hand tight. We stood there, in the middle of the well.

RUBY ELIZABETH SANDERS will spin the people around her. She will be the fixed point.

It was only a glint at first, the pinwheel. Then it came close enough to become recognizable. It skimmed and floated down one step, the next, the next, stopping to touch down once on each level, not bouncing but brushing, as if reminding itself of something. It dropped at Ruby's feet and I saw its colors. Striped metallic and liquid bright: the red of a cherry, the blue of the sea, the green of a leaf, the gold brown of Ruby's own eyes.

Which were on it, as it revolved.

It was for her. I took in a breath. This was the only thing it could have been. And I watched her reach for it, seeing herself here, at this center, where I had put her. What would her world look like as it spun?

AN INCESSANT DISCOURSE

by YURI HERRERA

translated by Lisa Dillman

LIKE ANY GOOD SCIENTIST, Doctor Aq knew that if a problem could be explained, it could be resolved, or at least avoided. That's why he was walking, by night, along an incandescent gorge, when all seemed lost.

Doctor Nt'ani had asked him to go to her lab to retrieve the discovery. The problem was how to find the place he'd been so many times before. It's not that there was no light on the street; there was plenty of light: from the buildings, glowing red- and white-hot. The contours of the city disappeared and were replaced by the contours of enormous embers, breaking off into blocks that became smaller and smaller and smaller, before turning to ash. A miner would be more use than a map, as far as finding his way. There were still people out on the street but nobody was saying anything: the time for shouting had passed. Or perhaps it was just that their shouts were scorched in the ether.

He managed to discern the heptagon of the science building, momentarily protected by the gardens aureoling the structure. Section four, to the left, housed Doctor Nt'ani's laboratory.

Doctor Nt'ani had spent the past several years in search of interstellar languages. If Earth had spent so long emitting signals on purpose, out of sheer irresponsibility, someone else might have too, and she was going to try to receive them, literally, up until the last moment. She'd formulated new equations in order to decrypt neglected corners of the world, something scientists do quite often, but Doctor Nt'ani was searching for pragmatic communication, a question. And she'd found it. A secret relationship between heat and light—not what they did visibly, but an appendix, a series of subtle patterns that had gone undetected because they seemed accidental.

"They've been communicating since the Mesozoic Era," she told him. "You have to go. The code for you to get connected is in the first book on the top shelf by the door. I can't go back now. I came home to get a computer and it's become impossible to leave. You go."

"But what did you find?" Aq asked. "How did they do it?"

"They left a form of artificial intelligence," Nt'ani replied, and the line went dead.

Twice he entered the heptagon and twice he reemerged immediately after feeling the drop in temperature. Though it was a relief, suddenly the lack of heat seemed abnormal; for a second it felt, absurdly, as if the danger were in fact on the inside. The third time, he kept going till he reached the lab. He hooked his computer up to the mainframe, located the book, found a page with the capital letters of certain verses marked up like an acrostic, translated the whole thing into numbers, and entered them. He waited.

The first thing to appear on-screen was his own image: red, covered in dirty sweat. What followed were many images that all looked like versions of the same image, but only later would he understand that this was not what it was. Then came shapes that might have been organic: tree branches or absurd diagrams, or rocks. And sounds—unintelligible, beautiful, shrill. Smells, though that couldn't be, what the... Combinations of images, sounds, smells, and a certain sensation, oscillating on his tongue and skin. Finally, one single pulsating image, the one that synthesized everything, impossible as it seemed.

"Got it?" came a voice like a muffled echo.

He waited a few seconds, and then said: "What took you so long to get in touch?"

"You're the ones who took so long to understand the message; we thought you'd get it far sooner, it took you ages to get it."

"Get what? What did I just see?"

"What you saw is what's been happening. Stories, histories. Senses, which are also histories."

"Technology?"

"No. Why would we do anything like that?"

"What appeared in that last image... Did you bring us that?"

"No. That's always been there, saying its piece. We just used it as a medium. You were the ones who should have deciphered it. You had so long to decipher it."

"But I don't understand; why answer us *now*?" He flung up an arm, signaling all around. "It's a bit late, no?"

The voice took its time to respond, as if struggling for an answer; it said: "Nor did we give you imagination."

He fell silent. The image of the flame stopped pulsating, then went out. Everything went out. Aq disconnected his computer and walked into the heptagon's corridors. On his way out, those first images flashed before him once more, embers, embers, embers, red and white embers, appearing as if before his eyes and not in his mind, as if the image were alive in his head; the sequence stopped on one, enlarged, and Aq began to see that those burning cinders were cities, that the one currently on view in his head was his own, his city, and that the particle moving in, out, in, out, of one ember— was himself.

He reached the exit. Opened the door to the heat that welcomed him back, stepped out, and began to read the encyclopedia of the universe before him.

BATTLE SCENES

paintings by CLAIRE BOYLE

The Lonely Hunter, 60" × 88", oil on canvas

Sweetie, 38" × 46", oil on canvas

Fleecer's Ball, 57" × 62", oil on canvas

Pet, 34" × 42", oil on canvas

Food for a Wedding, 119" × 66", oil on canvas

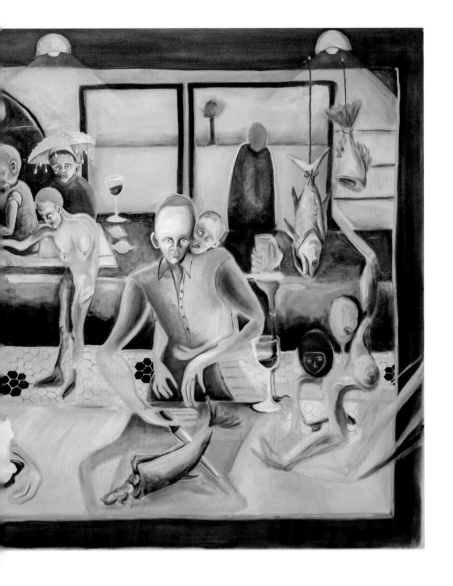

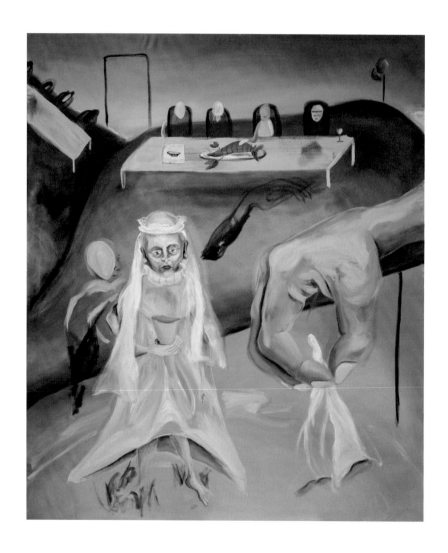

Hand Kleenex Bride, 58" × 68", oil on canvas

Peace from Nervous Suffering, 60" × 56", oil on canvas

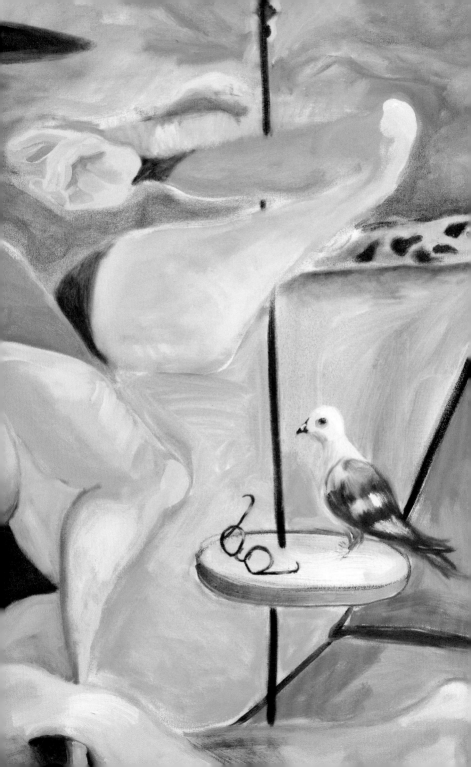

Dead Fish II, 22" × 38", oil on canvas

An excerpt from

PORTHOLE

by JOANNA HOWARD

I WILL NOT APOLOGIZE, I TOLD my driver. I am beyond apologies. They want me to work, they feel that I owe them work.

My driver remained mostly silent.

They think I will just pivot, but I won't pivot. If I could pivot, I would have done that years ago.

Who are "they"? the driver asked.

Everyone. The studio, my crew, the world.

That's what is called a consensus.

It was late in the summer, months after an accident on the set of my last film, and we were on our way to the asylum known as Jaquith House.

We curled on secondary roads through mountains covered in white pines along an enormous lake. Lupines bloomed on the roadside. We had been driving for several hours, the air growing steadily cooler and drier. I had not stopped talking for a second, or thinking audibly, as it seemed to me, and in fact there was little separation between my thoughts and my speech. I had become resigned to it, in the phase leading up to this exodus to Jaquith. I had come to expect phases. I was measuring my time not by film projects, as I once had, but by phases of breakdown. I knew it was happening. I had known it was happening even in the midst of the accident, I told myself I was on top of myself, but that was a lie. All I could do was watch the phases arrive and eventually pass. There had been the period of disorientation following the accident, and then the phase of crystal clear awareness, like the effects of a psychedelic drug, then eventually a merger of the two modes simultaneously. There had been the phase of absolute silence following the accident, then the phase of nonstop talking, then talking while silent. There had been the phase of nightmares, and then the phase of sleepwalking, and then the phase of insomnia, eventually the phase of sleeping while awake.

Mental health facility, the executives told me, a final shot at rehabilitating my film career, they said, and they would even pick up the tab: But what choice did they have? They were out on a note for one of my loose threads. They said it was about not attracting further bad press, but I had always been volatile, bad press was part of my draw. Yes, of late, there were other factors, I won't go into it. Keep me out of sight until I was back to myself, and then hold me to completing one last project. Then, of course, when that one final project is done, they can be done with me. That is what they think!

It's a wonder they want to help you at all.

It's for all the most superficial reasons, I assure you.

Money?

Cultural capital, awards. So-called acclaim—money is just the side effect.

An important side effect.

Or a harbinger of the death of art. Yes, I've made them money in the past, inadvertently—against my will—but I won't make that mistake again. They think they can pair me with an inside man, keep me on a short leash. Maybe I'd be more manageable. Collaboration, they say! Collaborationist, more like: that option! That ridiculous Spanish option. They are hemorrhaging. Anyone who knew anything about film has been put to pasture, replaced by venture capitalists. They have no idea what the future of film is, because there is no future for film.

At least you still have your…

My what? My health? My money? At least what?

Your looks?

Always one step behind. Beauty, they tell you when you are little, will get you everything. What a racket! And here I am again: not the lie, but where the lie has been. The great trauma of her life! I thought or said to the driver.

Whose life?

Mine!

If he had further thoughts, he did not dare voice them.

Well, I thought or said to the driver, a life of considerable confusion and lying!

Ms. Désir—try to close your eyes for now, he said. We'll arrive at Jaquith House in about an hour. "Restoration without demolition."

His voice was toneless, and when he spoke, I couldn't tell if he was asking a question or answering it.

Are you talking about the building or the method of treatment? Do you report to the doctor or the studio?

It's in the brochure. I'm freelance. Nowadays it's all about the gig economy.

I had not yet met Dr. Duvaux of Jaquith House, who was to be newly in charge of whatever I had become in this aftermath of the accident. I have never coped well with rapid changes.

What's your name?

In times of distress, the doctor advocates simplicity.

For your safety or for mine?

Just for simplicity.

We're all in it together? Far be it from me to advocate complexity, I said.

Relax, and stop talking.

The drive was breathtaking. But I was inured to breathtaking. I couldn't roll my eyes enough over breathtaking.

I watched a trembling mountain village scroll by, with a string of little false chalets. False chalet cafés and wineries, and little false chalets for ski-waxing and repairs, and little false chalet strip malls of littler, even falser structures selling high-thread-count linens or artisanal mustards, or fountain pens or aprons silk-screened with exotic goats, or real estate. Every third false chalet offered real estate. But beyond the little Xmas village, there was a rising mountain, the lake, dark, and then this lake gave off to another lake, an even darker, glassier and more expansive lake than the first, a type of lake district, for district seemed always to be the word attached to lake, while region is the word attached to coastal, and country the word attached to river. Or so it seemed to me. What did I know?

Stop talking. Just try to relax, he said.

Where are we? Have we crossed the border?

The doctor advocates remoteness. But we always stay close to the coastline.

Geographical fortification, I said. Against a coming plague. Think of it as a retreat.

Porthole *by Joanna Howard is forthcoming from McSweeney's in 2025.*

CÔTE DE NUITS

by JAMES KAELAN

AMELIA'S LAST NIGHT AT Anderson, with the wine director out sick, a middle-aged couple arrived five minutes late for their reservation. They looked a little out of place. The woman wore white slacks and open-toed, four-inch Louis Vuitton heels. She'd gotten a blowout that afternoon, and her ash blond hair looked blue in the marine light of the Chihuly chandelier that hung from the foyer ceiling like a giant anemone. Her blouse—Hermès, Amelia guessed, purchased from a discount reseller—was covered in short-brimmed equestrian helmets festooned with silk bows. The top was meant to signal that she rode horses. Judging by her husband, though, she didn't own a stable. He was jowly and red-faced and wore a golf polo with a TravisMathew logo on the collar. Almost certainly a developer from Escondido with a LOCK HER UP bumper sticker on his truck. He was the kind of man—rough, funny, casually racist, always ready to haul something for a friend in his Ford F-250 Super Duty—that Amelia's father got paired with at charity golf tournaments but would never invite over for dinner.

Amelia had discovered that she was good at ascertaining the wealth of Anderson's patrons. She felt nasty doing it, but as a sommelier, she found the talent was useful. Guessing wrong could be dangerous. For some people price was aphrodisiac; for others it was poison. Anderson was not just the only restaurant in San Diego with two Michelin stars. People came specifically for their cellar. They had Californian and Chilean and South African and Australian wines, of course. But they specialized in the Old World. On at least a monthly basis, a single four-top might order a flight of pinot noir from Domaine de la Romanée-Conti that totaled fifty thousand dollars. For what they were paying to get drunk, you could buy a foreclosed home in a lot of American cities and return it to the family who'd been evicted. But a bill like that might even put five hundred dollars in the dishwashers' pockets. Furthermore, as Amelia kept reminding herself, these people were having spiritual experiences. Domaine Leroy, for instance, following Rudolf Steiner's astrological calendar, gave each individual vine in its twenty-two-hectare vineyard a tea made from the fermented manure of a lactating cow, stuffed into a horn and buried for the winter on a south-facing hill. One of Amelia's clients, who'd ordered the 1996 Leroy Musigny Grand Cru for himself three separate times, claimed that the first two bottles had been dominated by grapes oriented toward Saturn, and that the third had been influenced by Mars.

"Which do you prefer?" Amelia had asked.

"Mars," said the man. "It tastes like I've just won a war."

Amelia waited in the hosts' alcove while Enrique described the five- and ten-course tasting menu for the couple. It was a Tuesday, and they'd made the reservation the night before for the only available table—a 9:30, near the bar—under Cartwright. A sudden, special occasion, Amelia assumed. Good news. But as she watched Enrique guide them through the late-spring offerings, Mr. Cartwright had a look of indifference on his face that bordered on disgust. He wasn't interested in the amuse-bouche of golden caviar and sea urchin. Even the deconstructed rabbit stew and the venison were probably too bizarre for him. He'd expected to order a thirty-two-ounce porterhouse with mashed potatoes. Mrs. Cartwright, though, looked from her menu to Enrique and back with the eagerness of someone choosing treatments at a spa: everything was its own exquisite, justified pleasure.

Amelia studied the body language at the table. Enrique asked Mr. Cartwright a question, and Mrs. Cartwright seemed to deflate a little at her husband's response. But she said something, Mr. Cartwright flicked his hand dismissively, and then she brightened again. This was good. She'd wanted the ten-course, he'd said five, she'd pushed, he'd given in. It was only a matter of one hundred forty dollars: two hundred sixty per person instead of one hundred ninety. But it said something about their vulnerability. If Mr. Cartwright hadn't relented they might've ordered a five-hundred-dollar bottle, split it bitterly, and left without ordering a digestif. Now, though, Amelia could determine the ceiling of the bill. And its height depended only on how well she could tell her story.

Enrique left the table and headed for the kitchen. Amelia caught his eye and he gave the little smile he always did when a table had consented to the big prix fixe, followed by a quick downturn of his lips and the simultaneous lifting of his shoulders—his shrug that said, *Take no prisoners*. Amelia's pulse quickened. Like Enrique, if it weren't for family meal, she couldn't afford to eat where she worked. Even her parents, a dentist and a COO of a medical devices company, would've balked at the median bill at Anderson—where the richest clientele possessed the treasure of kings. These royals had the personal number of the owner. You offended them at peril of professional death. But there were people like the Cartwrights, with large but limited amounts of money, who were, even in comparison to the conscripted infantry, fundamentally weak. They couldn't text Arthur Anderson and were despised by the oligarchs who could. That's what Enrique's gesture meant. He and Amelia had the power.

*   *   *

Amelia had started out at UC Davis as a viticulture and oenology major (before getting overwhelmed by organic chemistry and switching to English), and had for a long time believed there was almost limitless intrinsic value in the appreciation of fermented grapes. She still believed this, in many ways. The experience of sharing with your dearest friends a bottle pressed and fermented by a tenth-generation vintner did mean something. There was a spiritual compo-nent that you didn't find in beer. Most ales and pilsners and lagers went bad in a year. Liquor had an inescapably artifi-cial character—the consequence of its distillation. It didn't exist in nature. It was too powerful. It numbed rather than enlightened.

But wine was holy. Christ had drunk it. An elixir, but a humble one. Poured by princes at banquets, but grown and pressed by peasants. (Drunk in huge quantities by peas-ants, too.) Great grapes didn't need a lot of water, liked to be shocked by wild swings of temperature. The more stress they felt, the more complex their flavors. As fields of wheat succumbed to drought or flood, up on the rocky, south-facing slopes of arid hills near Adelaide and Córdoba and Alexandria and Paso Robles, gnarled vines would still produce their jewels. And under smoke-darkened skies, with cracks of gunfire in the distance, the faithful would gather, still, to drink their juices.

But the wine at Anderson—the unbridled excess of it—was vile. And Amelia had come, increasingly, to think of the prices as weapons. She didn't really care if someone enjoyed a twenty-thousand-dollar bottle. Her real satisfaction came from knowing that, lying in bed later that night, or staring bleary-eyed at their sagging reflection in the mirror the next morning, they felt ashamed—even if they wouldn't admit it to themselves. Her transition had been gradual. She'd graduated on the eve of the 2008 financial crisis and returned to San Diego to live with her parents. Getting hired at Anderson in 2009, first as a buyer, then as an assistant sommelier, and later, when she'd passed her Level 3, as the next in line to Victoria's throne at the head of the program, had felt like a series of heroic coups. The better part of a decade later, though, she hated what she sold. But to an exponentially greater degree, she hated the people who bought it.

Amelia waited for a few more moments, thinking about her tactic, and then made her way to the table. Anderson did not serve wine by the glass. It was a Tuesday, and though the Cartwrights were celebrating, it wasn't a weekend night, and they weren't with friends who might egg them on. The negotiation was between husband, wife, and sommelier. One—*maybe* two—bottles was all Amelia would have the capacity to sell. She could, of course, offer something from the bar. Getting a big martini into each of them might obliterate

their inhibitions. But then they might just order more cocktails and leave stumbling drunk with less than a thousand
dollars on their credit card, including tip.

With younger couples—under forty-five, say—Amelia
always addressed the woman first. With couples over fifty,
she started with the man. The age gap between sommelier
and client was wide enough that, even if the husband thought
he could sleep with Amelia, his wife didn't. But the man still
felt idolized. And that made him susceptible.

"Good evening," said Amelia, hands clasped behind her
back, smiling directly at Mr. Cartwright.

"Howdy," said Mr. Cartwright, his moist blue eyes
twinkling.

"Hi," said Mrs. Cartwright.

"I'll be your sommelier for the night," Amelia continued. "I don't know if you've had a chance to look over the
book"—the menu lay closed at the corner of the table near
Mrs. Cartwright—"but if you're here for a special occasion,
and you're looking for something really memorable, there are
a few bottles in our cellar that we only…"

"What beers do you have on tap?" Mr. Cartwright said,
cutting her short.

The question, and the timing, caught Amelia off guard.
She wanted to spit on him. Mrs. Cartwright, for her part,
seemed deeply embarrassed—like her husband had just
audibly farted. "Bill," she said, sounding somehow both
wounded and conciliatory, "I want to get a bottle. I want to

celebrate." She looked at Amelia. "I got my real estate license in January and I just made my first sale."

"Oh, that's amazing!" said Amelia.

If Mr. Cartwright wanted a beer, "*Fuck him*," Amelia thought, already doing the calculations. Even if the property was in Rancho Santa Fe, an acre of land without a house on it was going for nearly a million. A duplex in a retirement community might fetch three. If Mrs. Cartwright had dropped her commission to lock down a client, she'd still pocketed the better part of fifty thousand dollars. "Maybe I can show you something from a special list?" Amelia continued, directing all her attention to Mrs. Cartwright. "You only make your first sale once…"

"I'm going to look at the fancy wines, Bill," said Mrs. Cartwright. "I don't care. And you can either join me and have a great time or you can drink an IPA that you could probably get at Applebee's."

"I'll be back in just a moment," said Amelia.

If you were a little drunk, or if you wore glasses but had mislaid them, and you weren't familiar with the way stone flakes under a chisel, descending the steps into the cool belly of the cellar you might think you'd entered an Etruscan wine cave in Montepulciano. The walls were concrete, but fluted and furrowed by an expert trowel, and faux-painted with a delicate brush to look like hand-cut limestone.

The space, divided into two barrel-vaulted rooms, was fifty feet deep and twenty-five feet wide. Though the offerings were always in flux, Anderson stocked somewhere between twenty-five hundred and three thousand bottles arranged in regional factions—the Barolo and the vino nobile in one alcove, the Burgundy and Champagne in another, Australia grouped by state, California arranged by valley. The collection carried a separate insurance policy of fifteen million dollars; if anything, it was undervalued.

Looking over her matériel (what were these glass cylinders, frankly, if not munitions?), Amelia determined she would suggest something from the Côte de Nuits. Not only would Mrs. Cartwright probably feel comfortable with the varietal, but the list was also the heaviest in her arsenal. Among pinots that retailed for more than a compact car floated the cheapest bottle on the index: the 1995 Domaine de la Romanée-Conti La Tache Grand Cru Monopole, barely marked up from retail at eight thousand dollars. The 2007 Musigny, at forty-five thousand dollars, lay near the bottom of the ledger like the cornerstone of a great temple that had fallen into the Mediterranean. There was something perversely thrilling about showing someone, for the first time, the Côte de Nuits or Côte de Beaune or Rhône Valley lists. The prices were so incomprehensibly high that they reengineered your frame of reference. If you walked into Anderson thinking an expensive bottle cost eight hundred dollars, and then you suddenly discovered there were multiple recent vintages (not priceless relics exhumed, say, from Louis XV's tomb) twenty, thirty, or even forty times more precious, the corruption did not stem from the culture that rewarded such extravagance; the impurity was in your soul. *You are a sinner and you didn't even know it. Here is the word of God. You are saved. Bathe in this fount. Receive your absolution.* Through these wines, Amelia transformed people. *Those who do not know about this wine are your inferiors*, whispered the lists. *Those who do are your peers. Welcome to the world wherein the earth is not a limit on your spirit. Put your ear in the glass. That hum is the jubilant voices of banqueters at Versailles. The revolution will never breach the gates.*

Amelia crossed the dining room and handed Mrs. Cartwright the Côte de Nuits list. She didn't seem to balk at the numbers in the right column. But like Latin to the serfs, the words on the left meant nothing to this woman in and of themselves. And yet they were the very embodiment of grace. To speak them was to become one with God. Mrs. Cartwright couldn't do it herself. She was anesthetized by the French. Amelia would act as her intermediary. "Henri Jayer Echezeaux Grand Cru, 1990," she said, cantillating a prayer. "Leroy Domaine d'Auvenay Mazis-Chambertin Grand Cru, 1996."

Mrs. Cartwright made a low moan of pleasure.

"When Marc Benioff ate here, that's what he drank."

"Marc Benioff…," Mrs. Cartwright murmured.

"The CEO of Salesforce, yes."

"Salesforce…"

"It continues to open for hours," Amelia lilted. "The first note might be spring and wet earth and the new buds on the vine still acrid in the nose. Thirty minutes later it's full, hot summer. The bees are gathering nectar from the hills of lavender. An hour after that, months have passed. The days are getting shorter and the nights cooler. Now it's the sweet, musky grapes on the vines you're smelling, ready for harvest."

"Yes…," said Mrs. Cartwright. "Yes…"

The wine girl came to the table with the bottle wrapped in a white cloth laid along her forearm like a newborn. The waiter and two other men stood in a row behind her, watching as she cut the maroon foil and drilled into the bottle. After two deft levers of her tool, she broke the seal, twisted the stopper off the screw, ran the cork under her nose, and handed it to Caroline.

Caroline looked down at the little beige cylinder in her palm. With one end dyed a deep bloodred, it reminded her of a tampon. She had no idea what she was supposed to do. She looked across the table at Bill. He had a twisted little grin on his face. Either he thought this whole show was very funny or very stupid. Caroline was getting more embarrassed by the second. She could feel her cheeks growing hot. On the verge of panic, she lifted the cork to her nose and sniffed. It smelled normal as far as she could tell. Perhaps a little earthy, a little astringent.

The wine girl dispensed half an ounce into Caroline's glass, twisted the bottle a quarter turn clockwise to cut the pour, then dabbed the lip with her cloth. In the somber light of the restaurant, the liquid in her cup looked almost black.

Caroline was not prepared for the first sip. The last glass of wine she'd drunk, a Stella Rosa Red, had its own billboard on the 15 in Escondido. The d'Auvenay smelled like red wine, but in the first swallow she tasted dirt and salt water, burnt meat, rusted iron. If she'd been at home, she probably would've spit it out. But with the managers and the waiter watching, with the wine girl standing tableside in her cream blouse and fitted black blazer, her hair tied back in a high ponytail, a tungsten bulb in the ceiling forming a golden halo of light around her head, Caroline felt trapped—bewitched.

"Hold it in your mouth for a moment," the girl instructed. "Just notice how it expands, how it moves through the breadth of its profile, through all its flavors."

Caroline choked it down. "It's just not at all what I was expecting…"

She knew the bottle was too expensive to return. If she sent it back, Bill would tell the story at every Fourth of July, every Memorial and Labor and Veterans Day barbecue, every Thanksgiving, every Saturday round of golf, until he realized his ultimate fantasy and died of a heart attack on the eighteenth green at Temecula Creek. *She orders this one-hundred-and-sixty-dollar bottle of froufrou French wine*, he'd say a thousand times, *takes one drink, and sends it back. Last time I let her order*.

Caroline took another swallow and tried to find the French countryside. She closed her eyes. She might as well have been swilling pickle brine. She hated it. "Thank you," she said to the wine girl. "This is lovely."

"I'm so glad. I'll let you enjoy."

Caroline had always deliberately avoided wines that people described as funky or savory. It was very possible, she'd once joked to a friend, that everyone who said they liked these heavy, metallic flavors was lying; that somewhere in Europe a couple thousand years ago someone had said, as a joke, *I like that this tastes like mud, don't you?*, and for the hundred generations since, everyone had just been too embarrassed to disagree.

But Caroline was going to do her damnedest to be a good sport. After all, she was here to celebrate. Not only had she made her first sale, but when the inspector had reported that the roof would need to be replaced within five years and the buyer wrote for the full cost and threatened to walk if he didn't get it, she'd negotiated with his agent until they'd settled at ten thousand below offer. The little two-bed, one-bath Pala Mesa ranch still went for four hundred and seventy-five thousand—more than thirty thousand over asking. Even with her half-point discount she'd cleared seven grand. She and Bill might be swamped with more than a quarter million in credit card debt—to say nothing of their mortgage and the truck and her Tesla and the seven-hundred-dollar student loan payment she mailed every month to her daughter. But she could already feel the vise loosening.

Caroline took another drink. For a moment, balancing the liquid on her tongue and watching the legs cling to the crystal glass, she thought she was drinking a different wine. And in a sense, she was. The acid of unripe spring really was giving way to the lazy heat of summer. The farmers in the valley were cutting hay for the horses. The wild mustard still clung to its flowers. The sun didn't set till 10 p.m. and you could walk around in a sleeveless dress at three in the morning.

Caroline looked across the table at Bill. He was glancing down at his phone, hidden below the level of the table, frowning. He knew better than to mention it at a dinner like this, but the Padres had probably lost. She hadn't married him because he was fashionable or classy. He wasn't. The most formal clothes he owned, besides a couple of suits that he only wore to weddings and funerals, were his rack of Hawaiian shirts, his golf polos, and his moisture-wicking pants, which looked, from a distance, in the right light, like slacks. No, she'd married him because he was fun. He was a hard worker. And he'd turned out to be a good father. Harsh sometimes, but supportive. Starting when their son, Will, was four, Bill had coached T-ball and then Little League. When Will got to Temecula Valley High, Bill volunteered as the third-base coach. She didn't care that he didn't care about wine. Frankly, she didn't care about wine, either. There was old Bill, still grimacing at his phone, but she didn't feel any antipathy toward him. She loved him. It had been a tough couple of years. This meal was a deserved celebration, but it was almost certainly the most expensive night out they'd had since their twenty-fifth wedding anniversary. He was doing this for her. And he was probably starving.

Caroline put her nose into the glass and inhaled. It felt almost as if she were being lifted out of the room. She took another sip and felt the breeze that flowed up off the Mediterranean and over the Swiss Alps and down into the Côte de Nuits. She was surprised to discover that she had to fight back tears.

Amelia returned to the table eight times to pour for Mrs. Cartwright. (Mr. Cartwright, beyond comprehension, didn't partake.) By the time the bottle was empty and the couple had finished their dessert course—toasted-wakame ice cream infused with garden herbs and crowned with grilled honeycomb, blistered quince, and almond oil—and Mr. Cartwright had finally asked for the check, it was nearly midnight and the restaurant was empty. Enrique, the maître d', the chef de cuisine, the dishwashers, and Amelia were the only staff remaining. Everyone knew that the Cartwrights had ordered the d'Auvenay, and that they also didn't look like the sort of people who would order the d'Auvenay. The maître d', Gregory, couldn't help himself and pulled Amelia aside to double-check that she'd presented the menu—not just recommended the bottle out of context.

"Have you ever known me to act suicidal?" Amelia said, glaring at him.

"If you're wrong, just be glad Victoria isn't here."

"I'm not wrong."

But Amelia was nervous. And so was Enrique. They stood side by side in the semi-open kitchen, distractedly polishing silverware. The black book containing the check sat closed to Mr. Cartwright's left. Mrs. Cartwright picked up her glass and made a final toast. Mr. Cartwright lifted his half-full beer. He forced a smile. It was clear he was exhausted and nearly asleep at the table.

Finally, Mr. Cartwright opened the booklet, gave a perfunctory glance at the tally, closed it, tilted to one side to remove his trifold leather wallet from his back pocket, pulled out what looked to be a Capitol One Spark card (not exactly high-limit, but not necessarily a red flag), slid it into the little polyurethane sleeve, and stood the check upright.

"Well, that was easy," Enrique said, exhaling audibly. "Nice work."

"I hope so," said Amelia.

While Enrique went out into the dining room to collect the payment, Amelia distracted herself by thinking through what she wanted to drink when the shift officially ended. She wasn't at liberty to uncork anything from the imperial cellar. And, frankly, she wasn't that interested in any of the traditional, Old World reds she could afford. But there were two bottles in the staff wine refrigerator that she'd been waiting to try: a foam red pet nat from Austria, and a natural amber from the foothills that Enrique had brought. Amelia had introduced Enrique to natural wines. He still drank Tecate while watching the Chargers on Sundays, but on most Mondays he stopped by Clos to pick up something weird. She loved that about him.

Enrique passed by on his way to the computer. "If you're staying for a few minutes after," Amelia said, "I'll open one of our bottles."

"Claro," said Enrique.

Enrique's Queen of the Sierra amber was from Forlorn Hope. The winery had a PO box in Napa, but the grapes— mostly verdelho, albariño, muscat, and chardonnay—were grown in the limestone soil of a vineyard carved out of the manzanita in Calaveras County. This particular bottle was from an experimental batch. The vintner had added vermen- tino fermented for four months in a stainless steel drum with fifty free-range organic eggs.

The Vulkandame that Amelia had selected was made on a mixed biodynamic farm in the Austrian steppes. Vinovore, a new bottle shop in Los Angeles that focussed on female vintners, described the wine as a classic lambrusco that had gone on "an all night binger + got all crazy + wild ~ earthy black cherry cola dry." If the Cartwrights left peacefully, and Enrique didn't mind saving his bottle for another night, the sparkling red seemed the more jubilant of the two options.

Enrique emerged from the computer bay with a look of dread on his face. "Fun while it lasted," he said.

"Oh no," said Amelia, the back of her neck already tin- gling. "Declined?"

"Yep."

Her stomach tightened. She looked out the cut-through into the dining room. Either Mr. Cartwright didn't have enough space on the card, or the bank had flagged the purchase as fraud. As Enrique approached, Mr. Cartwright suddenly picked up his phone and answered a call. Enrique stopped twenty feet from the table, clasped the bill behind his back, and lowered his head to wait.

"Yes," Amelia heard Mr. Cartwright say. "Yes." Mrs. Cartwright was watching him, trying to figure out who her husband was talking to at midnight on a Tuesday. But as far as Amelia could tell, she didn't appear alarmed.

"Yes, I did," said Mr. Cartwright. "Well, I didn't look... I don't actually know." He paused to listen to the person on the other end of the line. Then he let out a loud pop of laughter. "The idiot must've forgotten a decimal point somewhere. Real glad you caught that. Yep, pull the hold... he's here... I'll tell him to run it again with the right total." He hung up and said something to Mrs. Cartwright and she put the back of her hand against her forehead and pretended to faint.

Enrique approached the table. Amelia couldn't hear what he was saying, but everything in his posture was deferential, almost juvenile. He was leaning forward, hunched, with slightly bent knees, clutching the check like it was a family heirloom he'd broken.

"You have got to be fucking kidding me!" Mr. Cartwright yelled suddenly. Amelia's heart began thumping against her sternum. "Let me see it." Enrique handed Mr. Cartwright the bill. Enrique wasn't speaking loudly enough that Amelia could understand him, but she could see him from behind, shaking his head. Her palms and armpits began to sweat. Mr. Cartwright's chair screeched as he thrust himself back from the table and stood up. He was shorter than Enrique, but he was barrel-chested and his thick arms stretched out the sleeves of his polo. He was right in Enrique's face. "You mean to tell me that bottle of fucking wine cost sixteen thousand dollars?! Are you out of your goddamn mind? I'm not paying for this. Carol, get up. We're leaving. This is fucking ridiculous."

Mrs. Cartwright sat paralyzed in her chair. Amelia, a dishrag in one hand and a butter knife in the other, couldn't move, either. Gregory, who must've been listening for raised voices, emerged from the hallway outside the manager's office, followed by the chef de cuisine, and headed toward the table. One of the dishwashers, Pablo, came up and stood beside Amelia. He didn't say anything.

Mr. Cartwright had turned bright red. "This is fucking fraud!" Now he was screaming at Gregory. "Are you expecting me to believe that my wife looked at a menu with a bottle of wine that cost sixteen thousand dollars and said, *Yeah, that's the one for me?* Give me a fucking break!"

"I could've read it wrong, Bill," Mrs. Cartwright was pleading. "I could've read it wrong!"

"You didn't read it wrong!" Bill shouted. "It's a fucking goddamn fraud! It's not about the money. I can pay the goddamn bill. I just ain't gonna do it. Sixteen thousand dollars for a bottle of wine?! I could buy... I could buy... I could buy..."

Mrs. Cartwright was sobbing now, palms pressed against her eyes, shoulders shaking.

"Where's the wine girl?" yelled Mr. Cartwright. "Let her come out here and tell me she didn't deliberately con my wife."

Amelia dropped the knife on the counter with a clatter and then interlaced her fingers to keep her hands from shaking. She squeezed so hard that the tips of her fingers looked red and swollen enough to burst.

"Pinche puto," said Pablo under his breath.

There had been blowouts at Anderson before. But they'd almost always been inter-party conflicts. Amelia had seen men knowingly saddle their tables with obscene debts as a kind of challenge, check transmogrified into asp. *Place this on thy breast. Dost thou lie still? Good riddance. Immortal longings are for the poor. My heaven is now. I can feel it pumping through my veins, the venom, the juice of Egypt's grape. But my lips art still warm, my cheeks rosy. Thou vanishest. This is thine dividend, my wine-numbed purple swollen cock in thy mouth, filling thee with piss whilst thy widow watches, wailing.*

Quite possibly, something miraculous was happening. Possibly, Amelia couldn't do this any longer. She tried to swallow. Fingers knotted behind her back, the knuckle of her right thumb jabbed into her tailbone, she dug the nails of each hand into the back of the other. Possibly, she was bleeding. Possibly, this was emancipation. She was standing in the dining room at this moment, a dozen feet from the table, and Mr. Cartwright was haranguing her. The bladder of fat under his chin was shaking. He was sweating from his bald head. He was plum-colored. He was spitting as he screamed. "This ain't ending the way you want it to!" she heard him yell. "I can tell you that. One way or another. It ain't ending like you want it to." He was laughing. "Oh boy, it ain't ending the way you want it to."

Amelia walked past the table; Mr. Cartwright kept howling at her; he was close enough to grab her by the throat; she was close enough to claw his eyes; she kept going, weaving among the other tables already preset for the first Wednesday seating, where she was scheduled to do this all over again; she went and pulled open the cellar door, entered, listened to the pneumatic wheeze as the hinged arm retracted to neutral; there were footsteps behind her, a voice; it might have been Mr. Cartwright, it might have been Gregory; she skipped down the steps lightly, the opening of a dance number, her right hip forward so she could land on each tread with the toe of her pump, choreographed to express confidence, the lightness of her freed soul; she began to whistle and the notes echoed around the man-made cave like birdsong. Then, grabbing them from the racks by their necks, one in each hand, she began to dash the bottles on the ground.

JUST A CALL AWAY

by MIEKO KAWAKAMI

translated by David Boyd

AN OLD WOMAN IS eating curry. Banging her spoon against her plate, and not in any normal kind of way. She's literally banging it against her plate. You're tempted to get out of your seat, walk over to where she's sitting, grab the spoon out of her hand, and throw it on the floor.

Then you have the sudden urge to have what she's having. But didn't you just eat a big lunch? What's going on? This isn't the way a forty-one-year-old woman should eat—it's way too much, way too soon. The smell of curry fills every corner of the café. The sound of the old woman's chewing invades your ears. Is the smell making you hungry? That can't be right. You're already as full as can be. You've got no appetite to whet.

You wouldn't be able to get anything else down. You think about what you just ate. You remember what's now settling in your stomach. Torn between gyudon and yakisoba, you went with door number three: the yakiniku bento that you ate on one of the benches in front of the train station. The salty-sweet sauce from the meat had leaked through to where the rice was and turned it brown. When you think about it now, the image in your mind seems somehow unreal, wholly unrelated to how it tasted—unrelated to your stomach, your memory. You go ahead and order the curry.

To your left, a woman is talking in a soft voice on her cell phone.

When you see the rings on eight of her ten fingers, you think she must be out of her mind. Why put on all that jewelry just to come to the café and whisper on your phone? You imagine what it would be like to confront her. Excuse me, do you mind? You know you're not allowed to talk on the phone in here, right? From above, the harsh light is hitting her on the forehead, right around her frontal lobe. You stare at her glistening, greasy scalp and think, Yikes, women can go bald too. You run your fingers through your own hair. She's still chatting away, speaking in a quieter voice now, all hunched over, maybe because you keep looking in her direction. Are you serious? Get off the phone, lady. If you said that, she'd either scurry out of the place or just sit there and ignore you—one of the two. But, you think, all the other customers here are blabbing, too, as loud as they please, but what, it's not okay if you're on your phone? Isn't everybody talking? If you were in her position, that's what you would say. You put yourself in her shoes and imagine defending yourself against your own attack. Why's it okay for them but not for me? If you can see the person somebody's talking to, then it's no problem, but it's wrong because I'm here on my own? No, you respond, the brain tells us it's abnormal when somebody's having a conversation without a partner. Do you understand what I'm saying? What you're doing isn't normal. And your voice doesn't help, either.

Your heart is racing. Maybe the coffee wasn't a good idea. You didn't even want it. No, that's not true. You just wish you hadn't had it. In the corner booth to your left, there's a bunch of women—older women—and from time to time they burst out laughing, really enjoying themselves. It irritates you. It's the middle of the afternoon, and the place is crawling with women with nothing better to do. The fattest of the bunch is gesticulating, holding forth in a loud voice. She's pasty and slovenly—the word *piggy* describes her perfectly, you think. She's got a purple scarf thing wrapped around her neck, so that makes her a purple piggy. You know, we're trying to find another place now. Sounds like she's talking about hospitals. I mean, I know he's alive, technically, but he's more dead than alive at this point. So maybe it's actually good timing. You take a gulp of water and replay the purple piggy's words in your head. Who's she talking about? Who's more dead than alive? You can hear the indifference in her voice, and it gets to you. Somebody she doesn't actually care about but needs to find a new hospital for. Somebody who's more dead than alive, dead to her. Meanwhile, the woman with the rings is still chatting away.

When the plate of curry lands on the table in front of you, you remember that you'd ordered something to eat. You check the menu for the price: 850 yen. You ask yourself why you got it. Seriously, why? A sigh wells up inside you. The more you exhale, the heavier your limbs and body get, that giant old ass of yours sinking deeper and deeper into the ancient seat you're sitting in—until the thing finally breaks, sending you ignominiously to the floor. You dig into the curry as if to paint over the image in your mind. Tears fill your eyes. You wash the curry down with water. Repeat. You grab the check, pay at the counter, and exit the café as if swimming through a crowd of people nobody else can see.

The wind's blowing. The sky is pale blue, stretching out as far as the eye can see, not a single cloud in sight. When it gets like this, you lose track of what season it is. Or what season comes next. Was it fall? Then, in the next moment, you realize it's spring. Right, it's spring. You didn't even want to go out, but you didn't have anything to eat at home, so you had to put your shoes on, lock the door behind you, and head down the cold stairs with one hand on the railing, all the while feeling like you were stuck in a fridge. You made your way to the supermarket by the station, but when you got to the automatic doors, you just couldn't do it—so you walked away with the yakiniku bento instead. And here you are now. It's spring, but the wind's so cold. It's spring, and yet the wind is so cold. The simple act of walking makes you feel like you're dragging something along with you, something hopeless, something pointless. But that baggage doesn't even belong to you. Who was it that gave this to you? Can you ever give it back? Can you leave it somewhere? Maybe you should just go home. As soon as the thought crosses your mind, you see the white background of the job sites, the registration pages with their tiny letters and little boxes that look like shredded bits of paper, and your mood turns dark. Your thoughts were more than dark enough to begin with, but now you realize there was even more darkness beyond that, and your mind floods with a darkness you never knew was possible. With nowhere to go and nothing to do, you keep moving. You go over the tracks. A train hurtles by. The same rush of metal, the same blinding streak of yellow, the same high-pitched noise in your ears.

You see a drugstore, and you think about masks. Maybe you should buy some. Like a moth drawn to light, you head inside to where the masks should be, but all you find is a message scrawled in marker: SOLD OUT, NO DATE FOR NEXT SHIPMENT. As you stare at those large round letters, you feel like somebody is spitting venom at you. Hey, dumbass, you thought you could just walk in here *now* and grab some masks off the shelf? Who, *me*? You scoff to yourself. Masks… What do masks do, anyway? Aren't they saying it doesn't make a difference if you wear one or not? I mean, nobody knows, right?

Even the so-called experts getting paid to go on TV can't seem to make up their minds, so who's the real dumbass?

You see a parent and child walking toward you. Mother and daughter. The mom is still young, her prettily made-up skin glowing in the light. A pattern emerges in your mind, a gingham in light pink—the pattern from your favorite outfit when you were about the girl's age. A short vest and matching culottes that were kind of pilled, but nice and thick. Perfect to wear around this time of year. In that moment, you remember an old photo where you're posing in that outfit next to your mom. That was spring too. How old was she then? You let your thoughts wander. And what happened to those clothes? You have no memory of throwing them out, but you must have outgrown them at some point, and after that they weren't your favorite anymore—so you could have gone a long time without noticing they were gone. Remembering is such a pain, you think. But the words don't come to you—more of a feeling. If you could just stop remembering things, then maybe you wouldn't feel half as blue, you think. Not in words, though—it's just an inkling. A burp sneaks up on you and the smell of curry fills your mouth. It makes you grimace. Then, a moment later, the pink gingham leaves your mind; you'll never remember that lost outfit ever again.

Bakery, post office, utility pole, dentist, corner, shrine, sign, parking lot. Walking in the opposite direction of your apartment, you name all the things that drift by on your left. You pass a couple walking a dog wearing a sweater. Across the road is a Christian kindergarten with a small church; you can hear children's voices in the air. By the school entrance is a big blackboard where they always write GOD'S MESSAGE OF THE DAY. You've never paid any attention to those messages, but just once you did wonder whose job it was to write those distinctive white letters. What kind of position did they have in the church? Was that an important job? Or was it just some menial task? Was there somebody who wanted that job, or did they just ask the person with the best handwriting? Did they get points or something for writing these things out day after day where people could see them? Points with God, maybe?

The wind gets stronger. No one can see it, but with every gust, the boundary between you and the world becomes a little less solid. The wind's eating into you, like river into rock, taking your cells away and carrying them somewhere else. How's it work again? Does the virus lose its power in the wind? You're thinking so hard you're making a face. A man your age, maybe a little older, walks by. He's obviously trying to avoid you, and he frowns right at you as he passes. Five steps later, you stop and turn around—then it hits you. Oh, right, I'm not wearing a mask. But how am I supposed to buy what nobody's selling? Then you start to wonder what would happen if you caught it. But it doesn't really connect. It's old people who are dying; it's old people who are at risk. So you probably wouldn't die, wouldn't be able to die, and even if you had to go to the hospital, you'd just end up having to leave again, tossed back into an unending series of days that are nothing but empty boxes. And even if you came down with a fever, you think, you wouldn't tell anybody. You don't owe anyone the truth, you tell yourself. You wouldn't go to the doctor, either. Living in fear—isn't that a form of punishment in itself? This whole situation is like a festival. People getting all worked up, making noise because they've got nothing else going on. But it isn't like that for you. It's not like you want to die, but you don't really want to live, either. You're not attached to death, or life, or anything. So no mask for you. What's the point? You just want to grab somebody, anybody, anybody with the desire to keep on living, and make them understand. But nobody will look you in the eye.

Just look at all these places, you think. Medical offices of every kind. Dentists, pediatricians, ophthalmologists, pharmacies. How many have you seen just walking around right now? It's not even that big a city, so who needs all these doctors? They're like fucking vending machines, all crammed together like this. Do the doctors know each other? Are they at each other's throats or what? Is the pandemic a good thing for them or not? Little clinics—too small for anybody to die in. You swing your purse with your phone and wallet around onto your back, shove your hands into your pockets, make your way over two crosswalks and turn right, then head down some street that's never meant anything to you and never will. You have no intention of going home, but your feet carry you in that direction. You've got nowhere to go. Nowhere else you can go. Your body knows it, too, but to make sure you don't notice, it throws in a few extra steps—so you can go on thinking you're free, on your own, unburdened by anybody else. It's just you deciding what to do, just you deciding to walk around like this.

You see a parked ambulance up ahead, waiting to be called into action, its white body looking even duller than usual. A bigger hospital comes into view, different than all the little clinics you'd seen on the other street. Now *this* is the kind of place where somebody could die. As you look at the building—its old brick walls, the spots of rust—you start to feel like you'd meant to come here all along. Then, borrowing all the routine and exhaustion of someone visiting a loved one, you step inside. At the reception window, the yellowish curtain is pulled shut; on the counter there's a tray for appointment cards and a shallow acrylic box filled with registration forms; in the waiting room—not the largest you've seen—there's nobody, not a soul. On the left is a set of stairs, and beyond that a hallway. A TV is hanging from the ceiling, tuned to a talk show with the sound off.

You sit down on one of the brown PVC sofas and pull out your phone. You quickly scroll through your social media accounts, running your finger over words and images you couldn't care less about. Thirty minutes pass in no time. You don't even realize how shallow your breathing is, don't even notice the stagnation, the depression it creates, settling low and heavy in your lungs like always. Time to go back, you think, and go to bed. Nothing has happened, and yet everything has disappointed you, betrayed you somehow. Tears form between your eyelids and your eyeballs; there's a knot in the back of your throat. The automatic doors open with an exaggerated noise and throw you out onto the gray concrete. There's no car there to send you flying—not here, not now. You go back the way you came. Behind the ambulance, next to the emergency exit, a woman is crying. She's got her phone up to her ear, and she's crying. There's nobody on the other end, you imagine. She's crying to no one. Because, even though you don't remember it anymore, you did the same thing a long time ago.

You go back to your apartment. Nothing's pushing you, but you rush into bed like you can't stand it any longer. The same old furniture, same old colors, same old curtains. Nothing else to see from where you are. On your back, you hold your phone up and fill your eyes with an endless stream of pictures from other people's radiant lives, all the words you could ever read and more. They're all the same, and they're all different; all bright, all painful. All dumb, all blind, all going along, all playing their part. You keep your eyes on the screen, and on that screen there's nothing you want to know or read, nothing you need to know or read, but you still can't peel your eyes away. With every blink comes another trickle of emptiness. As your eyes and head, your pores and organs fill up, you wish you could grab yourself by the legs, flip yourself upside down, and give yourself a good shake, clean out everything that's accumulated within you, wipe your inside out with a fresh cloth, and start over again—from the beginning. But you can't. It's not possible. You run the pad of your finger over the surface of your screen as if to push away your own reality, your own anxiety, forcing your eyes open as you wade through a punishing stream of other people's misfortunes, other people's announcements, other people's opinions and regrets, stuffing yourself full of these words and images that have nothing to do with you.

An actress who'd made a name for herself with her innocent image, someone who was later raked over the coals for having an affair with a married man, was now, several years after paying off the enormous amount of money she owed her agency, married to some successful businessman and apparently pregnant. They're building a luxury home in an exclusive part of the city—a home worth more than three hundred million yen. A woman in her thirties talking about her life making fifteen million yen a year. Satisfied? No way. I'd need at least twenty million to feel like I'm okay. The grand delusions of women in their forties dreaming of finding a rich and successful husband. Under every post, anonymous comment after anonymous comment—countless gripes, opinions, and all kinds of advice, some well meaning, some hard-hitting. Who wants to see that home-wrecker on TV again? Time to cancel her for good. You're just lucky—all of you—so stop looking down on people like you're so much better than the rest of us. When I got married, it was because

I truly loved my husband. Doesn't it matter who your partner is? When did the world get to be this sad? Take a hint. A rich and successful husband? That's the funniest thing I've heard all day… Who do you think you are? I mean, you don't even realize you're still single because you have no concept of how reality works. Your life is literally over. Same as always, you press LIKE on everything you read.

You sleep a little. Plug your phone in. You think about the invisible current flowing through the thin cord, and it reminds you of when you had that IV drip in your arm, a faint trail of blood making its way up the tube. You need to find another temp job, but while you've been telling yourself, Not today, you can do it tomorrow, a whole month has come and gone, and your armpits have been wet with nervous sweat the whole time. You don't dream. After two hours, you wake up with cold shoulders. You boil some water and eat a bowl of instant noodles. Then, looking at your phone, you learn that a certain author has killed herself.

It isn't the biggest news item of the last day or two, but it isn't the smallest, either, fated to appear on people's screens for a second or two before sinking into oblivion only hours later. But this author means more to you than that. The instant you see the headline, you actually think you're going to stop breathing.

You'd first read one of her stories two years ago. It was a shocking encounter, a discovery. You felt like her work said everything there was to say about everything—all the fears you'd ever known, all the fears you had yet to know, the things you'd never realized you'd lost, all the things you'd eventually lose... The kind of love you always hoped to have in your life. You became obsessed. She hadn't published that many books, but you'd read them all; you'd read *everything* she wrote, no matter how short. You'd read her interviews, too, and every article out there about her and her work. When you found out that the two of you had the same birthday, you felt the presence of fate—like you'd been struck in the back of the head with a blunt object, and in your rapture you heard a strange voice escape your own lips. You were sure you'd been born at the exact same moment, not even a second apart, and as you fantasized about what would happen when the two of you finally met, which of course you would, you sighed.

Half a year after you came to know about her, she joined Twitter out of the blue. At first, all she did was promote her own work, but over time she started sharing childish, desperate posts that didn't match up with her work or her personality. I can't sleep. I'm gonna have to take something. Ugh, all alone again. What's the point of life without real intimacy? Maybe true love means learning to forgive. I'm lonely. I'm so alone. So, so lonely. When is it going to end? You couldn't believe your eyes. Was the person putting all this out there for the whole world to see *really* her? But it was. You couldn't understand why she felt the need to write such asinine garbage, and it got to you. But the posts only piled up as the days went on, and an unending stream of mind-numbing exchanges with people who'd probably never even read her books started taking over your feed. In a barrage of posts straddling the line between fawning and pathetic, you learned everything you'd never wanted to know about her—sexual things, private things. Your phone trembled in your hands as you stared at your screen. What the hell is this? What's her deal? She sounds like... She sounds like... But you were too disillusioned to put the rest into words. Some author, neither famous nor nameless, with maybe a few thousand followers. Before long, she was writing impulsive, emotional tweets and replies that had nothing to do with her or her work, getting involved in endless debates and pointless controversies. She hadn't published anything new in a year. Soon your shock and disappointment shifted into anger and aggression. Then, two days ago, she took her own life. According to people who knew her, she'd been dealing with online abuse for several months.

You slurp the soup from your instant noodles, but you can't taste it. As soon as you realize it has no taste, the taste comes back, and you look around the empty room. You sit down on your bed, your phone clutched in your hand, and you go right to her account. The last thing she put up was a quote retweet: a response to a video of a puppy falling off a chair and then looking around with its tongue hanging out, a dazed look on its face. Poor baby! But how cuuute! Your heart is beating so fast and hard that it could burst out of your chest, but you don't even notice. You search for her name over and over, as fast as you can, poring over everything people are saying about her. So much venom. No wonder she killed herself. Come on, she was basically asking for it. She wasn't cut out for this, not even close. Like any of us are? I bet she was mentally unstable before she got here. She didn't kill herself. She got infected weeks ago. That's what got her. Wait, does that make her the first kinda famous death in Japan? Ugh, that's pathetic. Whoever it was that pushed her over the edge better lawyer up. There's no such thing as anonymity online. Obviously she was going through some stuff. But wasn't she way too old to be going online and airing all her crap like that? Somebody on here made her do it. If it was you, you can kiss your life goodbye. Murderer. You did this. Yeah, you—you, reading this right now.

You're so agitated it makes it hard to coordinate the movements of your finger with the movements of your eyes. You stare at your phone until your eyes go dry and start to hurt. It doesn't take you more than fifteen minutes to go through everything you can find about her, but you keep your eyes wide open and cycle through the same posts for an hour, two hours. Your ears ring. You swallow hard. Your knees are trembling,

so you get up and sit down again to shake it off. You bite your
nails. You delete your account. You turn your phone off and
toss it out of reach. Then, a few seconds later, you pick it up
again, switch it back on, and type in her name. No, this isn't
what you should be doing. You should go to the store and have
them cancel your phone—right now. No, it's too late for that.
Even if you can't see it, the data's there, and it's there for good.
Bile rises in your throat, and you feel like throwing up. But
whatever it is you'd need to get out to calm yourself down just
won't leave your body. You remember the words you directed at
her over the past couple of months. You can't remember everything, but there are some things you can remember exactly.
You shake your head. Saliva is practically pouring from your
mouth, but your throat is so dry it hurts; you fill your mug
with the tap water that you usually avoid because of its smell,
and swallow cup after cup. You feel like you've turned into
a pachinko ball. You remember a time when you were a kid,
sitting next to your mom as she fixed her eyes on the countless
little balls darting around inside the pachinko machine. You
were watching them, too, for what felt like forever. You start
to feel like one of those balls, like a mass of silver in motion.
Silver balls, hundreds and thousands of silver balls, multiplying and multiplying in a mindless trap, nowhere to go. Then,
in a cacophony of metal, the lifeless silver transforms into an
unrelenting, torrential force and descends upon her. Crushed
under its weight, she dies. You're still gripping the faucet, your
eyes on the dish soap, not even blinking.

* * *

You grab your purse and leave your apartment like you're being chased. You walk unsteadily through the night, but still make your way straight toward the station. The door of the café you went to earlier is glowing. You lean into it and feel it give way. The owner looks up at you for a fraction of a second, then looks away again and says in a voice devoid of any emotion: Take any seat you like... Any seat I like? What does that even mean? The words crumble as you drag yourself along, pretty much collapsing into the same seat you were in earlier. You grab your elbows and take one small breath after another. Then you recognize the person sitting next to you. It's the woman with rings on eight of her ten fingers—the one with the glistening, greasy scalp.

She's got her phone pressed against her ear. She's talking in a low voice, same as before. You open your eyes wide and stare at her. Sunken cheeks with no meat on them, bony fingers like birds' feet, bands on her neck so prominent you could grab them. You can't tell if she knows you're staring or not. Same as before, she's talking in a low voice, hunched over in her seat. You stare at her. You're not even blinking. I should make a call, too, you think. I should call somebody right now. But who? You can't come up with a single name. You look at the letters and numbers on your phone, but they don't take you anywhere, don't bring you anything, don't remind you of anything at all. There's nothing there looking back at you.

In the next moment, you find yourself tapping the woman on the shoulder. Hey, hi, excuse me, do you think I could borrow your phone? Who are you talking to? I love your rings, what are you talking about? So pretty, they're beautiful. But who's that you're talking to? In her surprise, the woman jumps back, grabs the nail clippers, notes, rubber bands, and balled-up napkins scattered on the table in front of her, stuffs them into her bag, and runs out of the café as fast as she can. You hear a ring as the door swings shut. You look at the phone in your hand. You touch your finger to the screen. It lights up, just once, as if remembering something, and then it goes dark again.

THE GOOD ONE

by VENITA BLACKBURN

I SLOWED FOR A YELLOW LIGHT when I saw my sister
pull her pants down near the bus stop to shit the curb. My
sister gave up talking to me in '09. That year she gave up
a lot of things, not just me: car payments, matching socks,
God, diamonds, sage in November, planning for tomorrow,
attending weddings/birthdays/retirements/baby showers/
funerals, pulling lemons off her neighbor's tree for cocktails
in the backyard, mammograms, listening to men tell jokes,
taxes, central air and heating, watching old cartoons, and some
other stuff. She still buys nail polish, deep purple like blood in
a vein. I saw her on the corner of Blackstone and Barstow Ave.

I came to a stop at the light and there she was with her ass to the concrete. For a second, I argued with my own memory, *No, that's not her. Yes, it is. No, no, no. You know and she would. She would. Yeah, she would.* And maybe I was proud of her for the first time since we were kids, because I wanted to give up shit in '09, too, leave all my garbage in a bag out on the curb to be eaten by machines at dawn.

Just before the light turned green a big blue truck moved around the corner and stopped in the street in front of my sister to call her a *nasty bitch.* She took out a cigarette and glanced at the sun. I wish we had fought more, had a better excuse to keep our distance, so I could say, *Yes, I'm the good one here and she did everything wrong and some people are like that, you know, bad inside, and when they can't pay their bills and have really bad acne, that's when you know.* Then I could make folks nod like they understand what I'm talking about, like they know I'm the good one when they tell me my skin is so clear.

Maybe we could try again. Maybe I could give up shame and vanity and beer with pie and washing my car every week and a daughter and credit cards and bike rides in the park and retinol and antiperspirant and TV subscriptions and eye exams and farmers' markets and parking tickets and maybe I got out of my car, took off my shirt and bra and panties, and pissed the crosswalk and then spat on that truck's exhaust pipe in a way that was both violent and sexual and people would say, *Oh, don't mess with that one, she's dangerous* and *hot* and *crazy* and *She might fight Jesus or the devil* and *Lock her up but don't get close.* Yes, *stay away.* Maybe the big blue truck didn't say, *You're fucking disgusting* and maybe it wasn't a whiny man's voice. Maybe it was a woman we both loved once and maybe she asked, *Do you need help?* Maybe she offered a card out of the window and a bottle of water and had no hate or fear in her eyes and smelled like witch hazel. Maybe she knew all the things people give away when their pockets and hearts get too small. Maybe all three of us glanced at the sun together, remembering that only dreams belong in space. Maybe we didn't glance at the sun at all but at each other instead and one by one whispered, *I missed you.*

The light turned green and the word *bitch* dropped from the truck like a punch line when my sister took the cigarette from her mouth, shiny purple nails sparkling, and blew smoke up to that blue truck's heaven and for a while, just a little while, I knew we still had a chance.

CLARE BEAMS is the author of the novels *The Garden* (Doubleday, 2024) and *The Illness Lesson* (Doubleday, 2020), both *New York Times* Editors' Choices, and the story collection *We Show What We Have Learned* (Lookout Books, 2016), which won the Bard Fiction Prize. Her short fiction has appeared in *One Story*, *Conjunctions*, *Ecotone*, and elsewhere, and she was a finalist for the New Literary Project's 2023 Joyce Carol Oates Prize. She lives and teaches in Pittsburgh.

VENITA BLACKBURN is an award-winning author of the story collections *Black Jesus and Other Superheroes* (2017), *How to Wrestle a Girl* (2021), and the debut novel *Dead in Long Beach, California* (2024). She is an associate professor of creative writing at California State University, Fresno.

DAVID BOYD is an associate professor of translation and Japanese studies at the University of North Carolina at Charlotte. He has translated books by Hiroko Oyamada (*The Factory*, 2019; *The Hole*, 2020; and *Weasels in the Attic*, 2022), Toh EnJoe (*Harlequin Butterfly*, 2024), and Tatsuhiko Shibusawa (*Takaoka's Travels*, 2024). Together with Sam Bett, he has translated three novels by Mieko Kawakami (*Breasts and Eggs*, 2020; *Heaven*, 2021; and *All the Lovers in the Night*, 2022).

CLAIRE BOYLE is a painter and editor based in Oakland, California. She completed her MFA in painting at the Art Institute of Chicago. Her work has recently been exhibited at the Jones Institute (San Francisco) and Color Club (Chicago). She served as editor of this magazine for six years.

JENNIFER S. CHENG is a multidisciplinary writer and artist. She is the author of the hybrid books *House A* (Omnidawn, 2016) and *Moon: Letters, Maps, Poems* (Tarpaulin Sky, 2018), which was named a *Publishers Weekly* Best Book of 2018. Her work has received support from Brown University, the University of Iowa, San Francisco State University, the National Endowment for the Arts, the US Fulbright Program, Bread Loaf, MacDowell, and the Academy of American Poets. *www.jenniferscheng.com*

EMILY CROSSEN's fiction has appeared in *New England Review*, *Ecotone*, *Black Warrior Review*, and *Zoetrope: All-Story*, where she received first prize in the Short Fiction Competition. She grew up in Pennsylvania and now lives with her family in the San Francisco Bay Area. She's at work on a novel.

LISA DILLMAN translates primarily Spanish-language fiction and teaches at Emory University. Her translations have won multiple awards, and she has twice been a finalist for the National Book Award in Translated Literature. Writers she translates include Yuri Herrera, Pilar Quintana, Graciela Mochkofsky, and Alejandra Costamagna. She is currently working on Cristina Cerrada's novel *Europa*.

CATERINA FAKE is an American writer and artist living in Paris.

SARA FAN received her MFA in poetry from the University of Illinois Urbana-Champaign and her MFA in creative nonfiction from the University of San Francisco. Her essay collection was shortlisted for the 2020 Graywolf Nonfiction Prize.

ELISA GONZALEZ is the author of the poetry collection *Grand Tour*.

SASHA GRAYBOSCII is a writer from Nebraska living in New York. Her short fiction has appeared in Electric Literature's *Recommended Reading, The Commuter* and elsewhere, and she's written nonfiction for the *Los Angeles Review of Books Quarterly* and *The Rumpus*. Her writing has been supported by the Kimmel Harding Nelson Center for the Arts as well as Alderworks Alaska Writers and Artists Retreat. She works in City University of New York writing centers and leads creative writing workshops for medical students.

YURI HERRERA was born in Actopan, Mexico, in 1970. His first three novels have been translated into several languages: *Kingdom Cons*, *The Transmigration of Bodies*, and *Signs Preceding the End of the World*, for which he shared with translator Lisa Dillman the 2016 Best Translated Book Award. That same year he received the Anna Seghers Prize at the Academy of Arts in Berlin for the body of his work. His latest books are *A Silent Fury: The El Bordo Mine Fire*, *Ten Planets*, and *Season of the Swamp*. He is a professor of creative writing and literature at Tulane University in New Orleans.

JOANNA HOWARD is the author of the novel *Porthole* (forth-coming from McSweeney's in 2025) and the memoir *Rerun Era* (McSweeney's, 2019). Other works include *Foreign Correspondent* (Counterpath Press, 2013), *On the Winding Stair* (BOA Editions, 2009), and *In the Colorless Round*, a prose collaboration with art-ist Rikki Ducornet (Noemi Press, 2006). She cowrote *Field Glass*, a speculative novel, with Joanna Ruocco (Sidebrow Books, 2017). Her work has appeared in *Conjunctions*, *The Paris Review*, *Verse*, *Bomb*, *Flaunt*, *Chicago Review*, *Brooklyn Rail*, and parts elsewhere. She lives in Denver and Providence and teaches at the University of Denver.

JAMES KAELAN is an innkeeper and the author of two novels: *We're Getting On*, which grew into a spruce tree if you planted it; and *999 Years of Peace* (excerpted here), of which only 132 copies were ever made, and which is currently wandering from reader to reader like a purloined library book. If you'd like to borrow one, just track down @cartoon_distortion and ask!

MIEKO KAWAKAMI is the acclaimed author of the international bestseller *Breasts and Eggs*. *Heaven*, translated by Sam Bett and David Boyd, was shortlisted for the 2022 International Booker Prize. Her most recent novel translated into English is *All the Lovers in the Night*, and her newest novel, *Sisters in Yellow*, is forthcoming from Knopf in 2026. She lives in Tokyo.

ICARUS KOH (they/she) is originally from Singapore and now lives in San Francisco with their cat, Momo. She has been asking the question "What does it mean to be human?" since she obtained sentience, and a conclusive answer has yet to be found. You can find their interactive-fiction mini-games, and their other work, through @ginsengsmoothie. This is her first published work of fiction.

CAILLE MILLNER is the author of *The Golden Road: Notes on My Gentrification* (Penguin Press, 2007). Her fiction has appeared in *Zyzzyva*, *The Southern Review*, and *The Best American Short Stories 2016*. Her essays have been published in *The Sun*, *Michigan Quarterly Review*, and the *Los Angeles Review of Books*. Her writing has been listed in *Best American Mystery Stories 2020* and *The Best American Essays 2017*. Her awards include the Barnes & Noble Discover Prize.

MATTHEW ROHRER is the author of eleven books, most recently *Army of Giants*, published by Wave Books. He is a cofounder of *Fence* magazine, and one of his tattoos has been featured in two books of literary tattoos. He teaches in New York University's creative writing program and lives in Brooklyn, New York.

JAN WILM (born 1983) is a translator and writer working in English and German. He has published a novel and a critical memoir on Ror Wolf in German, as well as a book on J. M. Coetzee in English; a short story collection and a book on tardigrades are forthcoming. In 2024, he was a fellow at the Santa Maddalena Foundation in Donnini, Italy. Based in Frankfurt, Germany, Wilm teaches translation at the Heinrich Heine University in Düsseldorf.

NELL ZINK is a literary novelist. She lives in Germany. Her next book, *Sister Europe*, will be published on March 25, 2025.

CLOSE
QUARTERS

Close Quarters members are a dedicated group of *McSweeney's Quarterly* subscribers who fervently believe that independent publishing is crucial for a culture of free, vibrant expression. Together, we're dedicated to telling the untold stories of our time, and providing readers with a sense of hope and adventure. McSweeney's publishes elegant books and periodicals that capture the complexity of the human experience, and our literary arts programs provide meaningful opportunities for readers, writers, and artists. Close Quarters members are one of the most important parts of what makes our work possible.

Join us. Donate via our online store, or, to learn more, please contact Amanda Uhle at amanda@mcsweeneys.net

Our heartfelt thanks to these Close Quarters members. They are cherished friends whose support is crucial to the work that we do:

Carli Cutchin	Jonathan Huang
Carol Davis	Jonathan Parker
Brian Dice	Gina & Dave Pell
Mark Fisher	Jessica Silverman
Brett Goldblatt	Caro Unger

McSWEENEY'S 73: MANIFESTO

McSweeney's three-time National Magazine Award–winning quarterly returns with a subjective and selective group of manifestos, all from the twentieth century and onward, all roaring with outrage and plans for a better world. Featuring life- and history-changing works from André Breton, Bertrand Russell, Valerie Solanas, Huey Newton, John Lee Clark, Dadaists, Futurists, Communists, Personists, and many more past and future -ists, plus brand-new work from brilliant radical thinkers Eileen Myles and James Hannaham. Let this incendiary collection light your whole world on fire. From the introduction: "We need manifestos. They are often strange, ill-considered, and regrettable. They are just as often brilliant and pivotal in changing government, art, and the direction of the human animal. But always manifestos are passionate, always they command attention and use language for perhaps its most urgent purposes—the rattling of complacent minds."

McSWEENEY'S 74

Coming to you housed inside a deluxe tin lunchbox illustrated by the legendary Art Spiegelman, *McSweeney's 74* features a portfolio of pareidolia art by Spiegelman himself, wherein he teases out images from random watercolor inkblots; original pieces by Lydia Davis, Catherine Lacey, and David Horvitz printed onto pencils; and three packs of collectible author cards, packaged in real tear-away baseball-card packaging and featuring some of the finest writers of our time, including Sheila Heti, Hanif Abdurraqib, George Saunders, Sarah Vowell, Michael Chabon, Eileen Myles, and many more. Find all this plus the official *McSweeney's Anthology of Contemporary Literature*: a book composed of some of the greatest works of McSweeney's past decade, with a new introduction by longtime editor Claire Boyle.

McSWEENEY'S 76: AFTERSHOCKS
guest-edited by Alia Malek

McSweeney's 76: Aftershocks presents a collection of contemporary Syrian prose—short stories, novel excerpts, and plays—that chronicles the literal and metaphorical earthquakes that haunt the Syrian people. Guest-edited by acclaimed Syrian American journalist Alia Malek, and encompassing the work of eight Arabic translators and sixteen Syrian writers (some of which have never before been translated in English), these contributors write across diasporic and refugee experiences, as well as from inside present-day Syria. In these pages, skeletons fall in love, Damascus alleys become time portals, letters tucked in bullet wounds reanimate the dead, minarets gush blood, and photographs become more human than humans. These stories ask us to imagine the unimaginable. They ask not "what is real?" but rather "how can this be real?"

McSWEENEY'S 75
guest-edited by Eli Horowitz

Guest-edited by longtime McSweeney's editor Eli Horowitz, our seventy-fifth issue contains ten radiant stories, each published as an individual booklet with stunning art by ten different artists. All ten booklets are collected inside a beautiful and sturdy and elaborately foil-stamped dossier-like case, which opens (rather extravagantly) to reveal a series of accordion pockets—each one containing a pair of booklets—and snaps shut (rather satisfyingly) with a magnetic closure. In these brilliant literary debuts there are fish guts, meteor hunters, military coups, ghost towns, and fake orphans. The stories, whose authors and settings span continents, dazzle in their originality of vision and voice. They announce themselves with bravado, excellence, and energy.

ALSO AVAILABLE
FROM McSWEENEY'S

ART AND COMICS

NONFICTION

HUMOR

COLLINS LIBRARY

ALL THIS AND MORE AT

STORE.MCSWEENEYS.NET

Founded in 1998, McSweeney's is an independent publisher based in San Francisco. McSweeney's exists to champion ambitious and inspired new writing, and to challenge conventional expectations about where it's found, how it looks, and who participates. We're here to discover things we love, help them find their most resplendent form, and place them into the hands of curious, engaged readers.

THERE ARE SEVERAL WAYS TO SUPPORT MCSWEENEY'S:

Support Us on Patreon
visit *www.patreon.com/mcsweeneysinternettendency*

Subscribe & Shop
visit *store.mcsweeneys.net*

Volunteer & Intern
email *bryce@thebeliever.net*

Sponsor Books & *Quarterlies*
email *amanda@mcsweeneys.net*

To learn more, please visit *www.mcsweeneys.net/donate*
or contact Executive Director Amanda Uhle at
amanda@mcsweeneys.net or 415.642.5609.

McSweeney's Literary Arts Fund is a nonprofit
organization as described by IRS 501(c)(3).
Your support is invaluable to us.